THE BOOKS OF GEORGE JEAN NATHAN

The Theatre

COMEDIANS ALL

THE POPULAR THEATRE

MR. GEORGE JEAN NATHAN PRESENTS

ANOTHER BOOK ON THE THEATRE

THE THEATRE, THE DRAMA, THE GIRLS

THE CRITIC AND THE DRAMA

Satire

A BOOK WITHOUT A TITLE

BOTTOMS UP

Plays

THE ETERNAL MYSTERY

HELIOGABALUS (*in collaboration with H. L. Mencken*)

Philosophy

THE AMERICAN CREDO: A CONTRIBUTION TOWARD THE INTERPRETATION OF THE NATIONAL MIND (*in collaboration with H. L. Mencken*)

Travel and Reminiscence

EUROPE AFTER 8:15 (*in collaboration with H. L. Mencken*)

Art and Life

THE WORLD IN FALSEFACE

THE WORLD
IN FALSEFACE

THE · WORLD
IN · FALSEFACE

GEORGE JEAN NATHAN

New York   ALFRED · A · KNOPF   Mcmxxiii

21485

CONTENTS

THE WORLD
IN FALSEFACE

I

No less than once a week I am asked by some otherwise amiable person why I, after all these years, persist still in consecrating my time and what measure of talent I may possess to a critical consideration of the theatre. "You have said your say," they tell me. "The theatre is too trivial for your later years. Why continue? Why not devote your effort to books on other and more important subjects?" I have been told this so often of late that it has begun to disturb me a bit. It is time, I conclude, to seek counsel with myself. Why, then, let me ask of myself, *do* I persist?

Performing, in the first volume of his "Prejudices," a critical phlebotomy upon me, H. L. Mencken made the following observation: "At the brink of forty years, he remains faithful to the theatre; of his books, only one does not deal with it, and that one is a very small one. In four or five years he has scarcely written of aught else. I doubt that anything properly describable as enthusiasm is at the bottom of this assiduity;

perhaps the right word is curiosity. . . . I sometimes wonder what keeps such a man in the theatre, breathing bad air nightly, gaping at prancing imbeciles, sitting cheek by jowl with cads. Perhaps there is, at bottom, a secret romanticism— a lingering residuum of a boyish delight in pasteboard and spangles, gaudy colours and soothing sounds, preposterous heroes and appetizing wenches." . . .

It is true that enthusiasm does not figure in my effort. I am, constitutionally, given to enthusiasm about nothing. But it is not true that curiosity is at the bottom of my effort. While curiosity is an habitual impulse with me, it has no part—or at best a very small part—in my devotion to the theatre. To the final indictment, however, I offer a plea of guilty, though with reservations. The theatre is, to me, a great toy; and upon the toys of the world what Mr. Mencken alludes to as my lingering residuum of boyish delight concentrates itself. What interests me in life—and my years have since he wrote marched across the frontier of forty—is the surface of life: life's music and colour, its charm and ease, its humour and its loveliness. The great problems of the world—social, political, economic and theological—do not concern me in the slightest. I care not who writes the laws of a country so long

as I may listen to its songs. I can live every bit
as happily under a King, or even a Kaiser, as
under a President. One church is as good as
another to me; I never enter one anyway, save
only to delight in some particularly beautiful
stained-glass window, or in some fine specimen
of architecture, or in the whiskers of the Twelve
Apostles. If all the Armenians were to be killed
tomorrow and if half of Russia were to starve to
death the day after, it would not matter to me in
the least. What concerns me alone is myself,
and the interests of a few close friends. For all
I care the rest of the world may go to hell at today's sunset. I was born in America, and America is to me, at the time of writing, the most
comfortable country to live in—and also, at the
time of writing, the very pleasantest—in the
world. This is why, at the time of writing, I am
here, and not in France, or in England, or elsewhere. But if England became more comfortable
and more pleasant than America tomorrow, I'd
live in England. And if I lived in England I
should be no more interested in the important
problems of England than I am now interested
in the important problems of America. My sole
interest lies in writing, and I can write as well
in one place as in another, whether it be Barcelona, Spain, or Coon Rapids, Iowa. Give me a

quiet room, a pad of paper, eight or nine sharp
lead pencils, a handful of thin, mild cigars, and
enough to eat and drink—all of which, by the
grace of God, are happily within my means—
and I do not care a tinker's dam whether Germany
invades Belgium or Belgium Germany, whether
Ireland is free or not free, whether the Stock Ex-
change is bombed or not bombed, or whether the
nations of the earth arm, disarm, or conclude to
fight their wars by limiting their armies to biting
each other. . . . On that day during the world
war when the most critical battle was being fought,
I sat in my still, sunlit, cozy library composing
a chapter on aesthetics for a new book on the
drama. And at five o'clock, my day's work done,
I shook and drank a half dozen excellent apéritifs.

Such, I appreciate, are not the confessions that
men usually make, for they are evil and unpopular confessions. My only apology for them is that
they are true. That is the kind of dog I happen
to be, and, I take it, a curse upon me for it! But if
some tremendous event were breaking upon the
world and men and women were shaking their
heads in terrified foreboding, I know myself well
enough to know that if I had an agreeable engage-
ment for the same evening I should keep it, were
the streets flowing with lava and the heavens thun-

dering forth their "Feuersnot." I speak, of course, figuratively, for if it so much as rains I do not challenge my comfort to the point of going out and getting my hat wet. What I mean to say, in plain English, is that if it rested with me to decide upon the fate of the West Virginia coal miners or to hear Fritz Kreisler play the fiddle, the West Virginia coal miners would have to wait until the next day. The Soviet theory of government doesn't interest me one-tenth so much as Gordon Craig's theory of the theatre. Whether the Methodists will go to heaven or to hell when they die doesn't interest me one-twentieth so much as Adele Astaire's dancing. And whether the Japs will conquer Los Angeles or Los Angeles the Japs doesn't begin to interest me one-hundredth so much as whether Anatole France's next novel will be as fine as his memorable "Revolt of the Angels." I am not glibly posing myself here as an "artist," an aloof, exotic and elegant fellow with a maroon bud in his lapel and his nose in the air. I am merely a man gifted, as I see it, with an admirable practicability: one who believes that the highest happiness in life comes from doing one's job in the world as thoroughly well as one knows how, from viewing the world as a charming, serio-comic, childish circus, from having a few good, moderately witty friends, from avoiding indigna-

tion, irritation and homely women, and from letting the rest—the uplift, the downlift, the whole
kit and caboodle—go hang.   Selfish?   To be sure.
What of it?

II

But what has all this directly to do with the
theatre?   The theatre, as I have said, is to me
one of the world's pleasures.   On such occasions
as it devotes itself to fine art it is one of the world's
genuine pleasures.   On such occasions as it devotes itself instead to the spectacle of Dutch comedians alternately kicking each other in the scro-
biculus cordis and falling violently upon their
amplitudina emphatica, it is a pleasure no less,
albeit of a meaner species.   It is, of course, not
to be denied that for one evening of real pleasure
in the theatre one often has to undergo a number
of profound tortures, but the same thing holds
true of the aesthetic satisfaction to be derived in
an art gallery, where bogus art is often no less rel-
atively in evidence than in the theatre.   One
reads a dozen new books before one encounters
one that imparts a glow.   One sits through a
dozen new plays before one encounters a "White-
Headed Boy," or a "March Hares," or a pas seul
by George Bickel—and through nine or ten dozen

before one encounters a "Caesar and Cleopatra."
To hold against the theatre on that score is to hold
as well against most of the other sources of human
gratification.

With all its faults, the theatre has amused and
improved the spirit of man for centuries on end.
Like the doll, it is the one toy that has outlived,
and will continue to outlive, the horde of attacking years. It has now and then risen to greatness;
it has now and then fallen to triviality—so have
literature, and music, and sculpture, and painting. William Shakespeare and Owen Davis,
Michelangelo and Paul Manship, Peter Paul
Rubens and Penrhyn Stanlaws, Johann Sebastian
Bach and Raymond Hubbell. There is no argument in contrasts; there are always contrasts. But
aside from the question of the theatre's place in
art, it remains that the theatre is good fun—and it
is of good fun of one kind and another that I
am, at the moment, speaking. My days are spent
professionally in the channels of literature—my
mornings with reading, my afternoons with writing. When evening comes, I am occasionally
very glad to have done with literature. Dinner
parties I can't abide; they bore me to death; I
never accept an invitation to one if I can lie out
of it. Drinking is amusing enough, but it is not
easy to find sufficiently amusing persons to drink

with. I am, furthermore, a bachelor and have no household duties to concern me, no wife to drive crazy, no offspring to play peek-a-boo with. Clubs no longer interest me. Every time I enter one, some terrible wet-blanket, preposterously overjoyed at seeing me again after so long an absence, rushes up to me, invites me to dinner on Wednesday at the other end of Long Island, and asks me to tell him confidentially if it is really true that Irene Castle is in love with her husband. I lost my taste for card playing some years ago; if I want to go to a supper party there are still four hours to kill; and the diversions that most persons favour in the intervening time do not especially quicken me. There is left, as Goethe agreed, the theatre. There is left, between the demi-tasse and the bedtime cigarette, this night "Romeo and Juliet," that night Sam Bernard, this night "Electra," that night Ann Pennington, this night a smash of beauty and that, a smash of slapsticks. A farce by the younger Guitry, an operetta from the Kärntner-Ring, a burlesque show down in Fourteenth Street, the monkeyshines of Robert B. Mantell, a Eugene O'Neill play, a touch of double meaning from Budapest, an unintentionally jocose English "society play," a tune by Oscar Straus, or Emmerich Kalmann or Victor Herbert, a Ziegfeld show, something by Dunsany or Synge or

Rostand or Thoma, a revival of some excellent
comedy or merely, perhaps, a trim ankle, a sudden, surprising, lightning flash of real poetry, a
comedian with an allegorical nose—one pays one's
money and takes one's choice. It is the grab-
bag nature of the theatre that makes it what it is.
It is not curiosity that takes me there, but hope.

But all this has to do with the theatre merely
as a diversion, and not as the peg for a writing
man on which to hang, as I have more or less
hung, a career. Pleasure is one thing, serious
work quite another thing. Well, let us see. The
theatre, as I look at it, is one of the best subjects
in the world from which to fashion a variegated
assortment of predicates. It is almost impossible
for the writer on politics to use politics as a hook
whereon to hang his opinions, say, of music or
cow diseases. The same thing holds true of
writers on music itself, or painting, or architecture,
or sports, or science, or archaeology, or economics,
or religion, or almost anything else save books.
The theatre, to the contrary, by the very nature of
its diverse constituent elements and its peculiar
ramifications offers to the man who writes about
it a hundred convenient opportunities to air his
views con sordini on nearly everything under the
sun, and what a writer craves are such opportunities. What is more, these digressions from the

main theme are not, in dramatic and theatrical
criticism, so patently or objectionably out of key
as they would be in other forms of critical ex-
position. Furthermore, if Mr. H. G. Wells is
justified in using the history of the whole world
to work off his implied opinion of Lloyd George,
I see no reason why objection should be made to
me for using a single line in a play by Mr. Samuel
Shipman to work off my opinion of unipolar in-
duction, sex hygiene, the political situation in
central Siam, or anything else.

For such meditations, the theatre provides an
admirably provocative field. One of the best
ideas I ever got for a digressive essay on humour
came to me while I was watching the characters
in a Strindberg play go crazy. The best essay on
Shakespeare that I ever composed was inspired
by a play written by the Hattons. My most valuable sardonic ideas on the labour problem came
to me while a two hundred pound blonde in strip
tights was being chased around the stage of a
fifty-cent burlesque theatre by an Irish comedian,
as the soundest theory I ever achieved on the flaw
in Regulus' African campaign in the first Punic
war was inspired by a shapely leg in a Gaiety
show. This is why my critical writings deal at
times with trivial and obscure plays and playwrights. The trivial is often the inspiration of

something that is not trivial. Shakespeare so en-
grosses the mind that it cannot wander, cannot
stray into other meadows. It is in the tensest
moment of a Broadway crook play that one phil-
osophizes upon the initiative and referendum, the
life and habits of the bee, the condition of the
babies in the southern provinces of Russia, the
art of Henri Emmanuel Félix Philippoteaux, and
the battle of Bull Run.

I am, of course, not so vainglorious as to imply
that what I personally am able to derive from the
trivial is always unfortunately also not trivial; I
address myself simply to the theory, which is, at
least in the instance of others more talented than
I, sound enough. The common notion that only
great art can inspire and produce great criticism
does not entirely convince me. Great criticism
often from little acorns grows. Dryden's "Defense of an Essay of Dramatic Poesy" grew out of
a third-rate preface to his brother-in-law's book of
fourth-rate plays, as his "Of Heroic Plays" and
"Defence of the Epilogue" grew out of Bucking-
ham's inconsiderable "The Rehearsal." Some of
the greatest criticism in Lessing's "Hamburg
Dramaturgy" grew out of completely negligible
theatrical performances. Goethe wrote imperishable criticism that grew out of plays by Kotzebue,
Raupach and Iffland, and some of Zola's finest

critical writing (*vide* "Our Dramatic Authors"
and, more particularly, "Naturalism in the Theatre") was inspired, during the years of his service
as dramatic critic, by the trifling exhibitions that
he was forced to sit through. Some of Hazlitt's
most pointed criticism in his celebrated "On the
Comic Writers of the Last Century" was derived
from such artistic immaterialities as Mrs. Cent-
livre, the actor Liston, and Cibber's feeble "Love
in a Riddle," together with such mediocrities in
playwriting as Bickerstaff, Arthur Murphy, Mrs.
Cowley, Charles Macklin and John O'Keefe. And
half of George Bernard Shaw's admirable critical
essays are founded upon such things as "Trilby,"
"The Girl I Left Behind Me," "The Sign of the
Cross," The Colleen Bawn," "True Blue," "The
Sin of St. Hulda," "A Night Out," "Under the Red
Robe," "The Sorrows of Satan," "The White
Heather," "The Heart of Maryland"—plays by
Sydney Grundy, Stanley Weyman, Marie Corelli,
Herman Merivale, Paul Potter and David Belasco
—French bedroom farces by Antony Mars, Drury
Lane melodramas by Cecil Raleigh, and leg
shows. . . . A thousand trivialities are placed in
the test tubes of aesthetics that a single piece of
sound criticism may endure. Ten thousand un-
known men die in battle that history shall record—

and the human race take inspiration from—the
name of a hill.

III

This, then, is one way in which I, hopeful of
worthy critical accomplishment on some future
day, look on the theatre. I do not deny, plainly
enough, that I might perhaps more profitably devote my efforts to writing on a subject or subjects
of conceivably graver importance to the world
we live in; some such subject, say, as a theory for
the improvement of the condition of the working
classes, or birth control, or civil service reform,
or international peace, or Peggy Hopkins; but I
know nothing about such things, and, as I have
already said, care less. What interests me are
not the troubles or problems of the world, but its
joys. Art, the thrill of beauty and the aesthetic
happiness of the minority are among these joys.
And in so far as the theatre can provide them,
the theatre engages me.

Life, as I see it, is for the fortunate few—life
with all its Chinese lanterns, and sudden lovely
tunes, and gay sadness. In so far as I have any
philosophy at all, it is founded upon that theory.
For the Nietzschean "Be hard!" I have no use,

however. It savours too much of cannon, thong
and overly intense purpose. For myself I substitute "Be indifferent." I was born indifferent;
and at forty I find myself unchanged in attitude.
When I read some enkindled yogi's indignations
over the slaughter of eight thousand Polish Jews,
or over the corrupt administration in this or that
country, state or city, or over the Ku Klux Klan,
the absence of true culture in Kansas, the riots in
Dublin, or the political machinations of the American Legion, I only smile, and wonder. Indignation does not make, and never has made, the world
any better than has my own objectionable philosophy of contentful laissez faire. No great man
from Jesus Christ to Stonewall Jackson has, in his
effort to make the world better, been fired by philosophical asperity and spleen. Rome, the greatest
nation in history, was never indignant about anything. Nor has been or is the nation of tomorrow,
Japan. The chronic indignation of France is rapidly driving her onto the rocks.

It is in this spirit that I seek the theatre as an
outlet for my ideas. An idea, on whatever subject,
seems to me to be more in key with my attitude
toward life if it is predicated upon an art. I like
the notion of that kind of ideational genealogy.
Art is, in the view of nine-tenths of the human
race, bootless, "unpractical." Thus, whether good

or bad, art provides an admirable postulate for
my philosophical snobberies.   Life, to me, is artificial; all my criticism of drama is based upon
the theory that drama is artificial life.   There
isn't so very much difference, in my way of looking
at things, between life as it actually is and life
as it is shown in the theatre.   I have often been
accused of this attitude by critics of my criticism,
and often been lambasted for it; I plead guilty
to the charge.   The theory that drama while admittedly mimicking life yet in some esoteric way
departs violently and absurdly from life is main-
tained chiefly by persons whose life departs violently and absurdly from drama.   "That isn't
true to life," said the Harlem shoe-dealer, as he
watched "Lord and Lady Algy."   "That isn't
true to life," echoed the flapper, as she watched
"Rosmersholm." . . .

Artificiality is often a premise from which one
may draw sound and ponderable conclusions.
There is no more logical reason why a sound philosophy may not be extracted from such variably
factitious a thing as a play by Björnson than there
is why a sound philosophy may not be extracted
from some such equally variable and factitious a
thing as the naturalist transcendentalism of Lorenz
Oken or the Kirkcaldyan gospel of unscrupulous
Mammonism.   If there is in all this an air of what

Mr. Burton Rascoe alludes to as the intellectual
practical joke that I frequently play whereby I
may have my little laugh on the reader, I hasten
to make assurance that it is the fault of my de-
fective writing alone, and not of my convictions.
That I am not always able, alas, to make the most
of the opportunities that the theatre and its drama
offer in this direction, that the ideas I am able to
develop from the artificiality of the theatre are not
often notable or even remotely interesting, is nothing against the doctrine and everything against
the meagreness of my talents.

Drama, to come more intimately to cases, is—
to me—one of the most interesting of the seven
arts. With music and literature, it appeals to me
more than all the others in combination. Unlike
sculpture and painting, it is alive. It is quick,
electric; genius in flame. It *is* literature: they
are Siamese twins. It *is*, in Shakespeare and even
in such as Rostand, music: music on the violins
of metaphor, on the 'cellos of phrase, on the drums
of rumbling adjectives and verbs. There is for
me a greater aesthetic thrill in the second scene
of Act II of "Midsummer Night's Dream" alone
than in all the paintings in the two Pinakotheks.
There is for me a greater aesthetic pleasure in
Synge's little "Riders to the Sea" than in all the
sculpture in the whole of Italy.

But, the argument goes, the theatre does not always, or even often, vouchsafe such agreeable and tonic reactions. Well, neither does the printed book page in literature nor the concert hall in music. If the theatre gives us a new Roi Cooper Megrue more often than it gives us a new Hauptmann, so the printed book page gives us a new E. Phillips Oppenheim more often than it gives us a new Joseph Conrad. And the concert hall gives us many more Vincent D'Indys and Tschaikowskis than it gives us Liszts. What man is there who wouldn't sit through fifty compositions by Erik Satie, Walter Braunfels, Harry von Tilzer, Tosti, Josef Suk, Rudolph Friml, Hans Pfitzner, Zdenko Fibich, Othmar Schmoeck, Elgar and Ravel if that were the price for hearing Chopin's scherzo in E major? And what man is there who wouldn't sit through fifty plays by Horace Annesley Vachell, Jules Eckert Goodman, Charlotte Chisholm Cushing, the Rev. Thomas Dixon, Wilson Collison, George Scarborough, Cosmo Hamilton and the Hattons if that were the penalty for seeing, on the fifty-first evening, Rostand's "Last Night of Don Juan?" Art, whatever her platform, is sparing, even miserly, with her genuine gifts.

But, unlike in the instance of the other arts where it is a case of art or nothing, a case either of aesthetic satisfaction or aesthetic irritation and disgust, the theatre is often immensely agreeable in an obscene way when it is not concerning itself with art of any size, shape or colour. When it is concerning itself with art, the theatre is at once great, noble and hugely delightful. When it is not concerning itself with art, the theatre is neither great nor noble, but it is often hugely delightful just the same. I have made bold to hint as much on a previous page. Mr. Charles Judels' lengthy description of his brother's prowess as an architect of superhumanly toothsome omelets in the show called "For Goodness Sake" has no more relation to art than it has to pleuropneumonia in horses, but it would take a peculiar idiot to deny that it isn't tremendously enjoyable for all that. August Wilhelm Schlegel would have laughed himself sick over it. And so would any other serious and important critic and art lover either before or since his time. W. C. Fields' golf game, Fred Karno's night in an English music hall, Harry Tate's aeroplane flight, Frisco's derby hat and cigar acrobatics, "Krausmeyer's Alley," the old Russell Brothers' act, Bert Savoy's Margie, Collin's and Hart's muscular nonsense, George Robey's painted nose, Ben-Ami's serious acting—of a thousand and one such things is the gayety of the non-art theatre composed. There is, in the theatre, a surprise ever around the corner.

It may be a great performance of "Hamlet," or it may be a good new blackface comedian—or it may be a memorable night of superb awfulness such as that provided by the play called "Survival of the Fittest" down in the Greenwich Village Theatre. Each, in its different way, is excellent diversion.

If one goes to a concert hall and hears a bad performance or to an art exhibition and sees only bad paintings, one's disappointment is complete. In the theatre, contrariwise, the worst play and performance of the year may provide the greatest hilarity. I have been going to the theatre professionally now for more than eighteen years, and the four most thoroughly amusing evenings I have engaged during that period were provided by as many exhibitions so excessively bad that they baffle description, to wit, the play named above, the showing of "The London Follies" at Weber's Theatre about a dozen years ago, the play called "The Sacrifice" written, produced and financed by a Brooklyn baker with his fat daughter in the star rôle, and the late Charles Frohman's production of Bataille's "The Foolish Virgin." Nor do I set down merely a personal experience. There is not a man who saw any of these who will not whole-heartedly agree with me. For the theatre is never more entertaining than when its effort to

entertain skids, and when the species of amusement
that it provides is not strictly of the species that
it has intended to provide. James K. Hackett's
Macbeth with the fresh shave, talcum powder and
round Milwaukee haircut, Mrs. Fiske as the six-
teen-year-old cutie in the first part of Edward
Sheldon's "The Highroad," Robert Edeson's glis-
teningly new patent leather pumps in the African
jungle scene of a Rida Johnson Young masterpiece, Louis Mann's professorial curtain speeches
expatiating upon the great literary properties of
the gimcrack in which he is at the moment appearing, Jane Cowl's society play in which the Knicker-
bocker club, the Ritz hotel and the Rolls-Royce
motor car are mentioned every few minutes and in
which the male guests at a fashionable town house
appear at breakfast—if my memory doesn't err—
in tennis flannels, the child actress as Mielchen in
the production of "The Weavers" at the Irving
Place Theatre who drops a piece of extremely intimate lingerie in a particularly tense dramatic situation, the Belasco adaptation of a Picard farce-comedy in which a chorus girl lives with a theatrical
manager for a month but modestly declines to
let him kiss her—find their match for sheer low
amusement if you can!

That, in essence, is the theatre as I see it; that,
the theatre to which I devote my pen, and with a

pestiferous catholicity of taste that embraces
"Medea" and "The Follies," Eleanora Duse and
Florence Mills. I do not take it very seriously,
for I am of the sort that takes nothing very seriously; nor on the other hand do I take it too lightly,
for one who takes nothing very seriously takes
nothing too lightly. I take it simply as, night in
and night out, it comes before my eyes: a painted
toy with something of true gold inside it. And so
it is that I write of it. I criticize it as a man
criticizes his own cocktails and his own God.

PART I

ART AND CRITICISM

§ 1

Criticism is the art of appraising others at one's own value.

§ 2

Great drama is the souvenir of the adventure of a master among the pieces of his own soul.

§ 3

Art states what we know in terms of what we hope.

§ 4

It has been said that great art is the product of trial and suffering. This is nonsense. The great artists of all time, even where they have been poor men sorely beset, whether psychically or materially, have with hardly an exception produced their masterpieces during the periods when a sudden turn of fortune, or a kindly patron, or an act of the gods has made life, at least temporarily, easy, peaceful and comfortable for them. Nor have they harked back to their days of trial and suffering, consciously or unconsciously, for the inspiration of their masterpieces. These masterpieces have almost invariably been the legitimate children of happiness of the spirit and material ease. Michelangelo's sacristy of San Lorenzo, the tombs of Giuliano and Lorenzo de' Medici, the Pietà di San Pietro, the David of the Signoria and the marvelous Battle of Cascina were born thus, as were all of the master works of Shakespeare and as were, too, some of the greatest of the compositions of Beethoven. If Shakespeare in later years harked back to the agony he suffered when his wife, in 1585, presented him with twins, it was only to reduce the incident to low burlesque in "The Comedy of Errors." Beethoven, beset by lawsuits and venereal disease, wrote the immortal music of his third period, including the Ninth Symphony and the grand fugue for string quartette, only after increasing deafness mercifully relieved him from listening to shyster lawyers and medical quacks, and from thus worrying himself to death. Well, they answer all this with the name of Dante. Dante, they tell us, conceived the "Vita Nuova" and "Divina Commedia" out of the ache of his baffled passion for Beatrice. A pretty tale. But the sordid facts are that, exactly one year and nine months after Beatrice died, Dante married his new girl, Gemma Donati, was apparently

equally in love with her, and wrote the "Vita
Nuova" and "Divina Commedia" not only twenty
long years after Beatrice had passed completely out
of his life, but also after what pain he might conceivably have suffered from his romantic worship
of the estimable, if aloof, future Mrs. Simone de'
Bardi was drowned to a very considerable degree
in the greatly superior travail incidental to the riots
of Florence, his banishment by the Neri, his disastrous political and economic failures, his home-
lessness and heart-sore wanderings, his grievous
disappointments, and his rapidly approaching
physical decay.

§ 5

The unmistakable trend of the theatre as an
institution is away from drama and toward comedy. This is inevitable. The cumulative sophistication of theatre audiences must soon or late delete
of effective drama many of the hitherto most valid
dramatic episodes and situations. The greatest
dramatist living today could not for a moment
make a modern audience believe—as Sardou
made an audience of the '80's believe—that the
villain who was chasing the heroine around the
table would actually seduce her right out on the
open stage. Nine-tenths of the essential and most

pulse-stirring situations of drama have already
worn out their power of suspense and excitation.
The audience of today knows in advance, and absolutely, that the hero is not going to be killed by
the villain, that the heroine is going to marry no
one other than the hero, and that the United States
Marines are certain to arrive on the scene before
the bomb goes off.   The amiable surprises of comedy alone remain as emotional apéritifs.   Drama,
in the commonly accepted meaning—which is to
say melodramatic drama as opposed to psychological and problem drama—is doomed out of its
own endless reiterations and out of the necessary
limits of stage realism.   For all the quarter-cen-
tury talk of realism, the only actual realism permitted the drama has been that which has been
confined, by public taste, decorum and faint stomach, to the wings.   The true realism of the
drama is for the most part found, upon reflection,
to have transpired off-stage and to have been reflected by and upon the prudently restrained characters immediately before the audience's vision.
From Ibsen to Hauptmann, from Eugene Walter
to Cecil Raleigh, the story is largely the same.
The characters on the stage merely speak realis-
tically of a realism of action that is for the
greater part made to play its course back of the
scenes.

§ 6

Expressionism is drama in the sense and in the degree that a telegram is a letter, or that the headlines of a newspaper article are the article itself.

§ 7

The critic is the business man of the arts.   There is small place in criticism for the dreamer of dreams.

§ 8

To speak of morals in art is to speak of legislature in sex.   Art is the sex of the imagination. In American criticism art is subjected to an æsthetic Mann Act.

§ 9

Great art has outlived a score of gods.   It is the only permanent and immortal religion.

§ 10

Gordon Craig's imagination is still patiently waiting for the modern dramatist to catch up with it.

§ 11

Sincerity, integrity of artistic purpose and emotional honesty are not essential to the production of sound and notable art. Consider the genesis of Shakespeare's "As You Like It," Ibsen's "The Master Builder," Edgar Allan Poe's "The Raven," and Thomas Jefferson's "Declaration of Independence."

§ 12

An actress should be, above almost everything else, beautiful. It is difficult to interest one's self in the passions and sufferings of a homely woman.

§ 13

Criticism is of three kinds: constructive, destructive, and what may be called condestructive.

§ 14

Among the Pilgrim Fathers who came over on the Mayflower to settle America there was not a single artist, or the son of an artist, or the grandson of an artist, or the great-grandson of an artist.

§ 15

The average modern play has three acts. Its contact with life generally ends with the first.

§ 16

In criticism, valour is often the better part of prudence.

§ 17

The drama lives for us the life of our neighbour in terms of ourselves.

§ 18

The actor is the maquereau of dramatic art.

§ 19

There can be no wit where there is not at least a measure of disillusion.

§ 20

Criticism may be permitted as many forms as drama. It may be in turn appropriately comic, melodramatic, tragic, farcical and burlesque.

§ 21

What is good taste? It is *anything* that a cultured man admires.

§ 22

Life is a conflict of principles. Drama, of emotions.

§ 23

Strindberg, the cynic, they sneer, was insane. Well, so was Schumann, the sentimentalist.

§ 24

The theatre lives by emotional sadism.

§-25

It is a mistake to call Wilde an artificial dramatist.   He was a realist of realists.   Only his characters, the mouthpieces of his searching realism, were artificial.

§ 26

"The passion of genius" is a bogus phrase. True genius is not passionate, but hard, cold, analytical, calculating.   Every great work of art is the result not of sudden flame and fire, but of reflection, meditation, and chill patience.   Dubious talent is passionate.   The mind and hand of genius are as sober and temperate as a bricklayer's.

§ 27

I can think of nothing more incongruous than watching "The Weavers" from a box seat.

§ 28

The useless always has an irresistible appeal for

me; that is why I devote myself to dramatic criticism, perhaps the most useless thing in the world. I have an unconquerable fondness for the purposeless luxuries of life, the things that are not practical, the little circuses of the soul and heart and taste and fancy that make for the merriment and pleasure of the race if not for its improvement and salvation. Years ago, in my nonage, I said to myself: "What is the pleasantest and most useless thing to which you may devote your life?" After considerable deliberation I concluded and replied to myself, "Dramatic criticism"; and I have since followed, and profitably, my own advice. For centuries men have written criticism of the drama in an effort to improve it, and with it the public taste. What has been the result? The "Frogs" of Aristophanes, written 405 years before Christ, has never been bettered in any way for dramatic satire; the "Iphigenia" of Euripides, written 425 years before Christ, in any way for profoundly moving drama; or the "Oedipus Rex" of Sophocles, written 440 years before Christ, in any way for stirring melodrama. The imperishable romantic drama of Shakespeare fingers its nose at all the dramatic criticism written before its time, or since. And in the matter of improved public taste the most widely successful play in the civilized world in this Year of Our Lord 1923 is a

crook mystery play by Avery Hopwood and Mary
Roberts Rinehart called "The Bat."

§ 29

Criticism should be written not for the dramatist,
the actor, the producer, or the public, but largely
for itself alone.   Generically an art out of an art,
it achieves authenticity as an artistic entity in the
degree that it weans itself from its sire and stands
upon its own legs.   In this way and in this degree
was Horace a greater artist-critic than Aristar-
chus, Cervantes a greater than Molina, Sir Philip
Sidney a greater than Ben Jonson, Dryden a
greater than Addison, Goethe a greater than Lessing, Voltaire a greater than Diderot or Beaumarchais, Zola a greater than Hugo, Dumas fils or Sarcey, Coleridge a greater than Hazlitt—and is
Walkley a greater than William Archer.

§ 30

Drama is literature.   But literature is not necessarily drama.   This is why good literary critics
often prove themselves bad dramatic critics.

§ 31

Strange hearts are moved most often by the
tremours of weak ones.   We are touched not by
dramatists who have dominated their emotions, but

by those whose emotions have dominated them.

§ 32

The drama may be realistic in almost every department save that of love, which is commonly held to be the field of its most realistic endeavour. If the average love-making scene out of life were to be placed on the stage word for word, gurgle for gurgle, and gesture for gesture, the audience would, after a few preliminary sardonic yawns, go soundly to sleep.

§ 33

The Viennese writes of love at 5 p. m. The Frenchman, of love at 12:30 a. m.

§ 34

If I were appointed official dramatic censor, I should, with negligible exception, promptly shut down every play that was doing more than $3,000 a week.

§ 35

All true art has in it something of impudence.

§36

Let us not revile American play reviewing too much. Look at the French!

§ 37

They talk of fine plays ruined by bad acting. Yet what is more odious than a despicable play improved by good acting?

§ 38

Let us in passing not forget to place a flower on the grave of "the dean of American dramatists," Augustus Thomas.

§ 39

The critic is worthy in the degree that his mind feels and his heart thinks.

§ 40

Art is not the meal of life; it is the appetizer. Only poseurs regard it as the former. Life without art would be indeed dull and tasteless, but life with art only would be sickening in its surfeit. There are other things in life than art, and some of them are equally beautiful, equally inspiring, and vastly more contributive to the health and happiness of the human soul.

§ 41

Satire is unpopular and unsuccessful in the theatre not because the public cannot comprehend it, but precisely because the public can comprehend it. What the public cannot comprehend very often proves a success in the theatre. Witness, recently, Andreyev's "He Who Gets Slapped," which not only the general public but the professional critic themselves, including myself, could not understand. Satire is unpopular simply because it is founded *upon* unpopularity. If it isn't unpopular, it isn't satire. Its very life depends upon its unpopular derision of everything that is popular. Popularity and attendant success are merely targets for its custard pies, each one of which contains a sharp slice of brick.

§ 42

I observe that the persons who speak of constructive criticism are those who speak of the late world disaster as "the war for humanity."

§ 43

Art never follows a flag.

§ 44

Even to the finest dramatic tragedy there is an air of demagoguery that irks me. The tragic dramatist has about him always more or less a trace of the moralist and exhorter.

§ 45

There is a type of critic that vaguely believes there is something about a pretty woman that prevents her from being as capable an actress as a homely one.

§ 46

Sudermann is a Hauptmann in lace drawers.

§ 47

The old critics live in the past. The young critics live in the present. The theatre lives in the future.

§ 48

There is probably not a single educated, civilized and tasteful man in all America who, though richly appreciating the mediocrity of "Uncle Tom's Cabin," hasn't gone to the theatre at one time or another in his life to see it acted. Than this, I can think of no better and no more convincing illustration of the pervading spell of the theatre.

§ 49

The moving pictures are worse today than they were eight years ago. This, I appreciate and thus

forestall objection, is not criticism. It is merely
a statement of fact.

§ 50

Has there ever been an actor who did not aspire
to be, at the same time, something else: a painter,
a writer, a social favourite, a musician—something
to make him, in the eyes of the world, not merely
an actor?

§ 51

His prejudices are the tipples with which a
critic reanimates his drooping talents.

§ 52

The foremost active producing director in the
theatre of today is Jessner. He makes all the rest
seem like children. With Reinhardt virtually in
retirement, there is no one to compete with him.
The influence of his remarkable imagination will
presently be felt all over the world.

§ 53

Much is made of the fact that I often leave the
theatre in the middle of the second act of a play.

Doesn't this prove my devotion to the theatre as nothing else could? If I didn't love the theatre would I, when the play is that bad, wait so long?

§ 54

Thought is not dramatic. Drama must therefore purge thought of everything but its active verbs.

§ 55

If the Le Bon theory of crowd feeling is true, the theatrical manager should take advantage of it in a direction that, thus far, he has overlooked. I refer to the matter of the seats in his theatre. These seats are at present constructed in such wise that they slant backward, and so cause the persons sitting in them to sink against the backs of the chairs. Accordingly, the general view of a present-day theatre audience, for all its interest in the play that it is watching, is of an assemblage of persons afflicted with a mood of languor and relaxation. That this aspect of the audience exercises its evil effect upon the variable number of its members who are, at best, already but moderately interested in the play, none of us who has

studied a theatre audience can doubt. Now, if
the manager saw to it that his seats were constructed in just the opposite way, that is, slanted
forward instead of backward, Le Bon would come
to his rescue post-haste. The audience would then
be pitched slightly forward, a sense and picture of
tenseness and rapt attention would be induced in
place of the current sense and picture of comfortable indifference, and the effect upon the
emotional recalcitrants would be instantaneous
and electrical.

§ 56

Constructive criticism has a lot to answer for.
Think of Maeterlinck!

§ 57

The greater the critic, the more he is criticized.
Ten thousand persons have found fault with Shaw
for one who has found fault with Brander Matthews.

§ 58

I never write a serious thing that some profound
idiot does not arise and say that I don't mean
it.

§ 59

Criticism of the arts consists in an intellectualization of emotionalism.

§ 60

The heroes of drama are not magnifications of the heroes of life, but reductios. No play on Napoleon has ever caught to any degree the size of the actual Napoleon. Stensgard of "The League of Youth" is merely a jitney Maximilian Harden, and Dr. Stockmann of "An Enemy of the People" but a miniature Senator La Follette. Lucio in "Gioconda" is D'Annunzio himself, but through the wrong end of an opera-glass. The hero of Tolstoi's "Power of Darkness" is a lilliputian Gorki. What stage captain of industry has equaled the late Charles Yerkes, what war correspondent of highly coloured stage melodrama Frederic Villiers? The Trigorin of Tchekhov's "Sea Gull" is Remy de Gourmont, Jr., the clown of "He Who Gets Slapped," a declension of his own dramatist-creator. Think of Manson in "The Servant in the House," and then of Jesus Christ. Go a step further. Think of Othello, and then think of Leutgert!

§ 61

Art demands oppugnancy, resistance, conflict. If unanimity of taste and opinion prevailed in the world, there would be no art.

§62

The critic who at forty believes the same things that he believed at twenty is either a genius or a jackass.

§ 63

The critic should never be indignant. If he be an acute and honest critic, he should not usurp for himself the prerogative of his readers.

§ 64

Indignation is the seducer of thought. No man can think clearly when his fists are clenched.

§ 65

Criticism is the avant-coureur of platitudes.

§ 66

What the moving pictures need are not more talented authors so much as more talented editors.

§ 67

Now that the Actors' Equity Association has affiliated itself with the American Federation of Labour, the art of Kean, Lemaître, Salvini, Coquelin, Irving and Booth has been duly exalted to a level with the art of the Cloth Hat and Cap Makers, the Wood, Wire and Metal Lathers, the Longshoremen's Association, the Amalgamated Meat Cutters and Butchers, the United Association of Plumbers and Steam Fitters, the Brotherhood of Tin Roofers, the Travelers' Goods and Leather Novelty Workers' International, and the United Upholsterers. The interpreters of Shakespeare in America are at last one with the Journeymen Barbers!

§ 68

There is, to the artist, often no criticism so humorous as that which fully endorses his intent and achievement.

§ 69

The hero of a popular play is always seen by the audience through the heroine's eyes.

§ 70

All great drama is a form of scandal.

§ 71

Beware of the critic who does not now and then contradict himself. He is a foe to the progress and development of art.

§ 72

Huneker is the only critic I know of whose position ever successfully survived an excessive employment of evidential quotations from the works of others.

§ 73

Criticism is the most aristocratic of the arts.

§ 74

In Congreve the talent of Sacha Guitry was genius.

§ 75

The drama of today is the comedy of tomorrow and the farce of the day after.

§ 76

One thin shaft of daylight streaming suddenly into a theatre would kill the greatest dramatic scene that a Hauptmann ever wrote.

§ 77

One grows weary of the constant reiteration, by novelists, critics and such, of the phrase "the meaninglessness of life." What do they seek in life and of it, these gloomy ones? Life, true, may be meaningless; but life is a great show none the less and, like all great shows, is properly, appropriately and happily, meaningless. What, may one ask of these dour fellows, is the meaning of a circus? Or of the "Follies"? Or of the Derby? Or of "Hamlet"? Or of Beethoven's seventh symphony? Or of Michelangelo's ceiling in the Sistine Chapel? Or of a pretty girl? Or of a bottle of Pol Roger 1911?

§ 78

To object to this or that man as an official censor of the arts on the ground that he is illiterate and an ignoramus is absurd. The object of all official censorship is to make the arts safe for the illiterate and ignorant portion of the public. It requires an illiterate and ignorant man to understand such a public, and to stake out the boundaries of its tastes.

§ 79

There are two kinds of dramatic critics: destructive and constructive. I am a destructive. There are two kinds of guns: Krupp and pop.

§ 80

Few artists have what is commonly denominated "the soul of an artist." The true artist's soul is often indistinguishable from that of one who is not an artist and whose life is devoted to more prosaic activities. The soul of an artist is generally to be found in an alien body, inarticulate, futile, and not a little grotesque. I have known

intimately many artists, all of them first-rate.
While their work may have breathed the soul of
an artist, they personally were psychically not to
be told apart from so many men in the street.
They did not look like artists, or talk like artists,
or dress like artists, or act like artists, or—out of
their studios—even feel like artists. Show me the
man with "the soul of an artist" and nine times
in ten I'll show you a man whose artistic achievement is negligible. Art is a practical thing. The
artist does not paint by moonlight or write in a
flower-bed.

§ 81

Of all the arts, criticism alone is made to suffer
from, and struggle under, a burden of good manners. This spirit of gentlemanliness that has been
imposed upon criticism has contrived to make it
the weakest and most backward of the arts. For
though good manners are held to be a desideratum
of criticism, there is none so nonsensical as to
maintain it to be a desideratum in any of the
other arts. There can be little authentic criticism if manners are insisted upon: sound criticism must most often inevitably be something
of a bounder. It is, for example, impossible to

write absolutely sound criticism of H. G. Wells
or of Cézanne or of Molnar's play "Liliom" that
is at the same time impersonal and hence well-
mannered. Take the case of Molnar and the
play referred to. How can criticism translate
exactly the present somewhat cloudy meaning and
intent of the play save it indulge in a boorish
pointing out of the impolite parallels between
the play and the life and the love of the man who
wrote it? Yet this means is by public voice forbidden to criticism. No other art is forced to
carry this millstone of good manners. Zola's "La
Terre" is as ill-mannered as a fashionable New
York stock-broker. The famous "Juno as a
Madonna" is as vulgar, in the conventional sense
of amenity, as Richard Strauss' obstreperous
"Zarathustra." Consider "Leda and the Swan,"
"Madame Bovary," "Die Götterdämmerung,"
"Œdipus Rex," the Venus di Medici, Rodin's
young marble lovers wantonly sucking tongues in
public without a stitch of clothing on. . . .

§ 82

Perhaps the most irritating thing in the life of
a critic of the arts is the fixed determination of persons to read motives into what he writes. I have

yet to write a highly unfavourable criticism of anything or anybody that some witling has not professed to find a motive therein. I have no motive save to write the most honest criticism that I am capable of. Yet if this honest criticism happens to find merit in the work of a friend or lack of merit in the work of an enemy, I am accused of favouring my friend and attacking my enemy. The truth is, perhaps, that a person capable of good work is my friend, and one capable of bad work my enemy. The motive-ferrets always read the sentence the other way 'round.

§ 83

All criticism is a form of envy: either envy that one could not do the thing as well, or envy that one didn't get the chance to do it a great deal better.

§ 84

The sound dramatist must have his share of humour, even if he keeps it hidden from his pen. But it must be in him none the less, to check him on occasion, to adjust his spectacles to the musing contemplation of the life around him, and to guard him against the temporary mists and clouds that, in their passing, seem stationary.

§ 85

Art is the child of ill health. In the whole history of art, there is negligible record of a completely sound and healthy man having produced a notable piece of work. Michelangelo, during the six years that he was working on "The Last Judgment," was a sufferer from violent intestinal disorders. Schumann was a victim of syphilis when he composed his finest songs. Rubens' "Fall of the Damned" was conceived and executed under the tortures of gout and neuralgia. Mark Twain's and Robert Louis Stevenson's delicate health is a matter of record. Lord Byron was born with a malformation of both feet. Stephen Crane suffered from acute alcoholism. Beethoven's sexual indiscretions brought with them a disease that remained uncured to the day of his death. Shakespeare, when he wrote "Hamlet" in 1600, had the gout. Heine was a victim of tuberculosis, and François Villon of the pediculus vestimenti. Goethe completed the second part of "Faust" in the rapidly failing months that ended with his death. Molière, though not a consumptive, had weak lungs that brought on frequent severe coughing spells. Strindberg was periodically insane, and Ibsen had diabetes. Swinburne's ailment everyone is familiar with. Rousseau's life was made miserable by delusions of persecution, brought to an end only by apoplexy. Mozart during the last half of his life was in feeble health that eventually affected his mind. Chopin had tuberculosis, and had to be nursed almost continuously in his later years. Swift's brain was diseased; he was subject to epileptic fits; "he was alternately in a state of torture and apathetic torpor." Cervantes, in the campaign against the Turks, was, in 1571, badly wounded at the battle of Lepanto, losing the use of his left hand and arm for life; his great work was all done in the subsequent years. Bach's eyes were so bad that he eventually went blind, his sight being restored only ten days before his death. Händel had a stroke of paralysis in one of his hands, and suffered frequent nervous collapses. Freiherr von Weber had consumption, and James Huneker had kidney trouble. Gluck had an excessively high blood pressure: it was apoplexy that finished him. Paganini had phthisis of the larynx and a constitution so delicate, from dissipation and from his custom of practising ten hours a day, that it could stand very little strain. Tschaikowski's serious illness up to the time that he was twenty-two years old left him in a very weak condition; he needed frequent long rest periods in which to gain enough strength to go on with his work. Samuel Johnson lost the use of one of his eyes from scrofula, and Verlaine spent month after month in hospitals. Sir Joshua Reynolds was deaf. Alfred de Musset, through irregular and dissolute living, was a weakling, and was able to work only three hours a day. De Quincey was an opium fiend, and got so bad that he had to take three hundred and forty grains a day. Homer, in his late years, was blind. So was John Milton, after 1652; he wrote "Paradise Lost" between 1658 and 1665; all his fine work was done after his eyesight was gone. Robert Greene, the English novelist, dramatist and poet, suffered for years from violent indigestion: he died after eating pickled herring. William Cowper in early life showed symptoms of melancholia: his attacks of suicidal mania led to his frequent temporary confinement in private asylums. Saint-Saëns had to give up his residence in Paris because of certain pathological idiosyncrasies. Nietzsche had bad eyes and suffered from ceaseless headaches. He also had constant stomach trouble. Richard Strauss' lungs have bothered him for many years. Lafcadio Hearn was a chronic invalid; he had the constitution of an ailing woman.   Victorien Sardou would never have written the plays that made him famous had his health not been carefully looked after by a charitable neighbour, Mademoiselle de Brécourt. Even Anthony Trollope had gallstones. . . .

§ 86

The business of the theatre and its drama is to quicken either the mind or the memory, the heart or the pulse.   Drama must do either one or all of these things, or it is not drama.

§ 87

A man I have difficulty in understanding is the one who, falling within the field of my criticism and meeting with its disapproval, becomes wroth at my written estimate of him and, even more so, at me.   Surely were the tables reversed, were he the critic and I the victim of his findings, I know myself well enough to promise that I should view both his criticism of me and the man himself without irritation or anger.   Yet hardly a month passes that some writer whom my appraisals have exasperated does not either publicly revile me as a fellow fit only for the society of dogs and worms, or send me a violently abusive letter.

As I say, I can't understand such a man. Certainly I, in my approaching two decades of literary, critical and editorial life, have been subjected to as much criticism as any analogous man I know. Nine-tenths of this criticism has been unfavourable, and a goodly share of the nine-tenths has been decidedly derogatory. Yet I have never felt, spoken or written—so far as I can remember— a single irascible reply, even when I had reason to believe that there was an axe somewhere in my critic's woodpile. I know my faults as well as the best of my critics, and I have so many of them and they are so obvious that once in a while even a mediocre critic cannot escape smelling out one or more of them. I am not perfect, I know full well; and I thank God that I am not. For if I were, ambition would naturally leave me, and I should give up the struggle of writing that affords me such tormenting pleasure, and doubtless spend the rest of my days drinking too much, playing nonsensical golf, sitting around my club, or chasing after flirty women. Harsh criticism, whether just or unjust in my own opinion, keeps me at the wheel; it challenges me; it keeps my blood dancing; it makes me fight, not my critics, but myself. And no man ever hit another upon the nose more often and more tellingly than I hit myself. I am, constitutionally, an æsthetic

Marquis de Sade, with myself as the subject of my endless critical flagellations.

But the man who grows red in the face and sputters like a new garden hose when he fails to meet with my critical approbation—I cannot grasp him. Does he believe himself perfect? I doubt it. No man, not even a recognized donkey, goes so far as to believe that of himself. Does he believe that I am dishonest in my attack on him, and is so perhaps justifiably indignant at me? Again, I doubt it. For, though I have been accused of many things, many of them true, no one, so far as I have heard, has ever accused me of not being honest. I have no reason to be dishonest. I have never belonged to a group of log-rollers; I am a bad mixer, so called, and dislike what passes for personal popularity; I fortunately have enough of the world's goods not to want more; I have enough friends; I never ask a favour, nor do one if I can avoid it; I am approximately as temperamental as a cold potato. There is thus no intelligible reason why I should be dishonest. Dishonesty could avail me nothing, be of no benefit to me in any conceivable way.

But if the man whom I criticize adversely does not believe himself perfect or me dishonest, what reason has he for being worked up? Does he believe that I am ignorant, and unable to detect

the merit that has on this occasion eluded me?
Possibly. But if he believes that I am ignorant,
why is he aggravated? No intelligent man, or
even partly intelligent man, can imaginably become exercised over what an ignoramus has to
say of him or of his work. If I am, to him, a numskull, why shouldn't he dismiss me with a long, loud
laugh? . . . Well, one reason remains for our
friend's irascibility. Does he believe that I am
intelligent, and that I have detected the truth
about him; and is it this exposé that makes his
ears burn? If it is this, then he is an artist without gratitude and without self-esteem, for the
truth should make him stronger once he is privy
to it, and his future work better and finer and
sounder. If he grows angry over what he knows
to be true, he is simply a damned fool.

§ 88

Each of us has his prejudices that will not bear
scrutiny and analysis. Many of these prejudices
are wholly without rhyme or reason, yet nothing
can subvert them. They are the blind spots of the
mind and soul, senseless, idiotic, yet immovable
and unchangeable as a wall of stone. Take, for
example, my own. I can't abide orchestral music
in the open air. There is no reason why the

"Egmont" overture al fresco is not as compelling as the "Egmont" overture indoors, yet there is something about it when it is played out of doors —at a Stadium concert, for instance—that invariably impresses me as baroque and futile. Again, the prose of Gilbert Murray is excellent prose, yet I can't comfortably read it. I try to read it; I know that it is meritorious; but I don't like it. And I can't figure out why. Still again, there are Gobelin tapestries. The best of them fail to move me; they all look exceedingly ugly to me; I wouldn't, so far as my personal taste goes, give ten dollars for the most priceless of them. Still again, Hauptmann's "Hannele," an excellent piece of imaginative dramatic writing, impresses me as burlesque. For all my consciousness of its merit, I feel myself snickering at it. In the same way, I have a senseless prejudice against stock-brokers. I know two or three who are very fine fellows—well-educated, companionable, men of good taste and considerable charm. Yet I can't be friends with them: there is something about them—I don't know what—that I don't like. Then, also, there are Romain Rolland, silk underwear and the "St. Sébastien" of Augustin Ribot. There is something to be said for each. But, for all that I know it, I can't bring myself to a proper appreciation.

§ 89

Of all forms of theatrical entertainment, melo-drama possesses perhaps the greatest intrinsic integrity. As the stage is designed primarily to exaggerate and intensify life, so melodrama is similarly designed. Thus, more exactly than comedy, tragedy, farce, or satire, does melodrama meet the demands of the stage. Comedy touches life too closely to come within the accurate, fundamental, unadorned principle of the theatre. Tragedy is but another form of comedy, a paraphrase, so to speak. Farce exaggerates life, but does not, by virtue of its humours, intensify it. And satire is, obviously, not a pure theatrical form. Melo-drama alone meets the theatre's every law and by-law. It is the blood of the stage.

§ 90

It is the custom of the critic of heavily mature years, in commenting on the views and attitudes of the younger critic, ironically to allude to the latter's youth, and condescendingly to observe that this youth is responsible for the "impuritan" ideas that in later years the critic will doubtless ponder and recant. The ancient, so writing, writes truer

than he knows.   But the truth has a boomerang
up its sleeve.   When I get to be old, I, too, shall
undoubtedly do my share of such condescension
toward the young critics, but I wonder if my writing thus will fool me?   I wonder if I shall retain
enough of my humour secretly to realize that what
I thus write will be only by subtle way of subconsciously apologizing to myself for getting old,
and losing all my erstwhile passion and fire and
courage and enterprise, without which criticism
is an empty art, and life an art more empty still.
I pray that I shall not try, at the expense of thus
gaily deceiving myself, to deceive the readers of
my sixty-five-year-old critical writings into believ-
ing that I am still alive and kicking.

§ 91

I quote from *The Dial:*

Mr. O'Neill begins with the stokers' bunks on a liner,
the air, the language, the emotions equally thick; and
with lapses to be noted proceeds through a gradual con-
ventionalizing of things, and a slow abstraction of
emotions, to a climax in which he presents as something actually happening, the phantasms of the protag-
onist's brain.   From that point on it does not matter
how "real" anything appears; *what matters only, as
always in the theatre, is what is effective.*

Who will deny that, so far as mere effectiveness
in the theatre goes, "Lightnin'," for example,
doesn't "matter" ten times more—and isn't therefore by *The Dial's* standard a greater work of dramatic art—than, say, Heijermans' "The Good
Hope" or Hauptmann's "Michael Kramer"?

§ 92

Although there doesn't seem to be much sense
in the remark, I yet believe that fine music and
fashion somehow do not jibe. I do not believe
that one can get full pleasure out of fine music
when one is all figged out. Beethoven can't be
profoundly enjoyed in a swallow-tail, or the songs
of Schumann in décolleté. Fashion is all right
for the banalities of the operatic stage, but truly
beautiful music and negligé go best together.

§ 93

It is impossible for the true critic to be a gentleman. I use the word in its common meaning, to
wit, a man who avoids offense against punctilio,
who is averse to an indulgence in personalities,
who is ready to sacrifice the truth to good manners
and good form, and who has respect and sympathy
for the feelings of his inferiors. Criticism is in-

trinsically and inevitably a boorish art. Its prac-
titioner takes colour from it, and his gentlemanliness—if he has any—promptly becomes lost in its
interpretative labyrinths. The critic who is a
gentleman is no critic. He is merely the dancing-
master of an art.

§ 94

Impressionism and Expressionism.—Impressionism: the expression of an impression. Ex-
expressionism: the impression of an expression.

§ 95

American criticism suffers greatly from the fact
that it is written by Americans. The American
critic, for all his brave effort not to be, is a cowardly critic. He is fearful of his position in the
community, of his neighbour's opinion, of the
opinion of his potential prospective employers, of
what will be thought of him tomorrow by someone
whom he doesn't know today. I know whereof I
speak. I am an American critic. And I had to
fight with myself long years before I achieved my
present—and even still but comparative—integrity.

§ 96

The words theatregoer and playgoer are all too commonly regarded as synonymous. Often they are not. A playgoer is one who goes to the theatre with the express and definite intention of seeing a play. A theatregoer is more often one who goes to the theatre in the spirit that one goes on an outing, that is, merely for a change, to get out for diversion from routine. The play is the least important thing that draws him to the theatre.

§ 97

Governmental censorship of the arts in America, and of the theatre in particular, is—for all the indefatigable eloquence of its opponents—bound sooner or later to become a reality. Nothing can stave it off. Where is the American still so foolish as to believe that his taste in art will not eventually be subjected to such a censorship when his Federal Government has already subjected to official censorship his taste in tipple, amour and travel?

§ 98

In a review of one of my critical lucubrations, the estimable Mr. A. B. Walkley, of the London *Times*, takes me to task in the matter of a detail. "The article," he writes, "is a plea for the emancipation of criticism from every kind of 'law,' on the ground that art itself has been emancipated, and criticism is only art of another kind. Upon this I would suggest to him that criticism is art in *form*, but its *content* is judgment, which takes it out of the intuitional world into the conceptual world."

A question. Is not such literature as, say, Mr. Wells' "The New Machiavelli," like criticism, art in *form* and its *content* judgment?

§ 99

Sound art is never recondite. Molière and Shakespeare are as transpicuous as Maeterlinck and Georg Kaiser are ambiguous. That a great work of art is susceptible of many meanings, many interpretations, seems to me to be largely nonsense. What, tell me, are the *many* meanings, and *many* interpretations, of "Romeo and Juliet," Haydn's "Kindersymphonie," Raphael's "Sposalizio," or the "Divina Commedia" of Dante?

§ 100

The essence of music show entertainment consists largely in the feeling that one is superior to the human beings providing it. As humour most often lies in the discomfiture of the other man, so music show entertainment lies in one's sense of the relative inferiority of its participants. If, for example, one's father, wife and best girl were simultaneously to get up on the stage and kick each other in the ribs, one wouldn't be particularly amused. But if, on the other hand—the act done —their places were to be taken by a clergyman with a bulbous red nose, an actress with a sizable bustle and Dr. Henry Van Dyke and these were to indulge themselves in the same jocosity, one's amusement, inspired by one's unquestionable sense of superiority, would be guaranteed.

§ 101

Let the moralists, when they revile the sex dramatists, not overlook the boldest, the most conspicuous, the most indefatigable, and the most dangerous of them all. I allude, obviously enough, to God.

§ 102

That great critics often contradict each other is no argument against the value and estate of criticism. Great artists also often contradict each other, yet is the fact ever used as an argument against the value and estate of art? If Goethe contradicts Schlegel, Wagner contradicts Mozart, and if Zola contradicts Sarcey, Cézanne contradicts Manet, and Ibsen contradicts Sardou. Go further. What if great critics often contradict themselves? Do not great artists often do the same? Consider the Hauptmann of "Henry of Aue" and the Hauptmann of "Rose Bernd." Or the Richard Strauss of the "Wanderer's Sturmlied" and the Richard Strauss of "Don Quixote." Or the Laurence Sterne of "Sermons" and the Laurence Sterne of the "Sentimental Journey." Or the Mark Twain that everyone recognizes and the Mark Twain of "The Mysterious Stranger" and "What is Man?"

§ 103

The fact that dramatic criticism in America is ridden with sentimentality finds fresh illustration in the current extravagant eulogies of the histrionic genius of the late Bert Williams. Whether Williams was or was not the great actor that my colleagues claim he was, I have not the vaguest means of knowing, since he did not give any definite indication of exceptional talent during his life-time, and since table-tapping doesn't convince me. Save for his familiar, excellent poker game pantomime (which was essentially a vaudeville act), I never saw him do anything (possibly because no manager ever gave him the chance) that had anything to do with acting, whether good or bad—and I saw him do everything that he did do from the early days of Williams and Walker to the day of his death. To hear him sing a single comic song was to hear him sing a hundred: he never varied his method in the slightest; he was as monotonous as a metronome; he exercised no ingenuity or imagination; he ceaselessly rolled his eyes by way of scoring a point in exactly the same manner that Raymond Hitchcock gives a dry cough or that Sam Bernard adjusts his trousers. The hypothetical genius of Williams was a legend fostered in the sentimental critical hearts by the circumstance that he was a negro and hence, it was somehow imagined, a theatrical under-dog. Did he not travel in a separate coach when he went on the road with the white members of the "Follies"? Was he ever elected to the Lambs' Club? Had he not wistfully behaved himself—unlike Jack Johnson—and confined himself to a black wife?   From all of this it was a simple step to endow him with virtues histrionic as well as ethical.   If he had been a white actor, he would have been treated critically as any other white actor, but, being a negro, he was sentimentalized as American dramatic criticism sentimentalizes, and thus confuses the artistic values of, four things out of five: as with old age—in the instance of, say, Mrs. Thomas Whiffen; as with heroic war service—in the instance of, say, Mr. Allan Pollock; as with unselfish and worthy endeavour in fields removed from the theatre—in the instance of, say, Miss Elsie Janis; as with death at an early stage in a career—in the instance of, say, Mr. Harold Chapin; and as with an alien struggling bravely with the native tongue—in the instance of, say, Mr. Jacob Ben-Ami.

§ 104

They ridicule George M. Cohan for his cheap habit of waving the flag.   They may, if they are so inclined, on the same score ridicule Euripides and Shakespeare.

§ 105

Censorship is birth control applied to art.   It

seeks to prevent artistic conception by introducing the whirling spray into æsthetics.

§ 106

If you ask me to name the three finest prose stylists that America has produced, I turn my attention from the field of professional letters and give you the names of Thomas Jefferson, Aaron Burr and Abraham Lincoln.

§ 107

Much nonsense is written of the "ennobling influence" of great art. What precisely, for instance, is the ennobling influence of half of the greatest dramatic art from the time of Sophocles to the present day? What is the exaltation of the spirit induced by "Œdipus"? Or by "Lysistrata"? Or by the "Rudens" and "Menaechmi" of Plautus? Or by "The Tempest," "Macbeth" and "Othello"? Or by the "Polyeucte" of Corneille and the "Mithridate" of Racine? Or by the finer dramas of the Restoration? Or by the "Belisario" of Goldoni? Or by "The School for Scandal"? Or by Schiller's "The Robbers" and "Wallenstein"? Or by Ibsen's "Rosmersholm" or "Ghosts," to mention but two? Or to come up

to our own day, by Strindberg's "The Father,"
Hauptmann's "Colleague Crampton," "The Recon-
ciliation" and "Gabriel Schilling's Flight," Galsworthy's "Strife," Tolstoi's "Power of Darkness,"
Gorki's "Night Refuge," Tchekhov's "The Sea-
gull," and Schnitzler's "Reigen"?

§ 108

Of all the arts, painting is perhaps essentially
the most feminine.   It is, at bottom, sculpture in
rouge, lip-stick, powder, mascaro, belladonna and
henna—lying flat upon its back.

§ 109

I am customarily accused of being a destructive
critic.   I fear that I can't summon up sufficient ingenuity to disprove the charge.   Let me, therefore,
and with creditable shame, make a full confes-
sion.   Looking back over the eighteen years of
my critical writing I find, to my eternal damnation
in the eyes of my worthy constructive brethren,
that I have, so to speak, worked my wicked will—
among others—upon such eminent petitioners and
suitors of fame as these: Charles Klein, the realistic hocus-pocus of David Belasco, Augustus
Thomas, the Gertrude Hoffman version of the Rus-

sian Ballet, the drama of Hall Caine, the genius of
Otis Skinner, "Bought and Paid For"—the Play of
the Century, the Oberammergau bootlegging of
Charles Rann Kennedy, the artistic aims of the
Actors' Equity Association, Maeterlinck's mysti-
cism, the brilliant white flame of Samuel Shipman,
Russ Whytal, the Corinthian soul of Percy Mackaye, "Abie's Irish Rose," the propaganda drama
of Brieux, the profound art of Henri Bernstein,
Sophie Tucker's vocal accomplishments, the match-
less talent of Stanley Houghton, the length of Mr.
Henry Kolker's trousers, the wit of the Hattons, the
eerie fantasy of the later J. M. Barrie, German
plays whose scenes were transferred to Hawaii and
which were then announced to be the work of Irish
playwrights, Sydney Grundy, Cizzie Fitzgerald's
wink, the æsthetic motives of the Princess Theatre
during its posture as the American Grand Guignol,
the ormolu Shakespearian fairies of Granville
Barker, the intellectuality of Mrs. Fiske, the remarkable genius of Edward Sheldon, the Drama
League, the art of John Luther Long, Clayton Hamilton's bleeding heart, the geist of William Vaughn
Moody and of Israel Zangwill, vaudeville (both
American and Russian), Emanuel Reicher's John
Gabriel Borkman, the art of Butler Davenport, Mr.
Louis Mann as a pundit, "Mrs. Warren's Profes-
sion," the librettos of George V. Hobart, the plays

of George V. Hobart, the lyrics of George V. Hobart, Schaeffer—The Most Versatile Genius In The World, dramaturgic rules, the New Art of Owen Davis, the "religious atmosphere" of four out of every five Biblical plays, the philosophy that Sarah Bernhardt is every bit as young today as she was sixty-five years ago, the glory of Bronson Howard, Ridgely Torrence as a great dramatist of negro life and character, the art of the movies, the drama of Robert Hichens, Lou Tellegen, J. Hartley Manners' five-foot shelf, the trip to the Neighbourhood Playhouse, and Alice Delysia's stentopgiæ. . . .

I blush, and hang my head.

§ 110

The average modern American play is to be appraised in the person of the actor who plays its hero.   Both confuse an artificial coat of tan with intrinsic robustness and vigour.

§ 111

Arthur Hopkins rejected Molnar's "Liliom" on the ground that it contained a scene depicting Heaven as a courtroom, which, he argued, would offend many persons.   Yet five years ago Mr.

Hopkins produced the Macphersons' "The Happy Ending" which contained a scene depicting Heaven as a platform covered with green cheese-cloth and peopled largely by members of the Lambs' Club.

§ 112

The negro is the fine music show entertainer that he is because the negro belongs to what is essentially a music show race. His mind—taking him in the aggregate—is a libretto, the clothes with which he is fond of adorning himself are scenery, his general deportment is to the general deportment of the average Caucasian what Mr. Ned Wayburn is to a Baptist minister. One seldom sees a negro or a negress on the street that one doesn't vaguely expect the former momentarily to go into a clog dance and vaguely feel that the latter is on her way to buy a second-hand red, green and yellow dress covered with spangles.

§ 113

Men go to the theatre to look. Women to listen.

§ 114

1. Not to go to the theatre is like making one's toilet without a mirror.

2. If a second or third rate play is performed by second or third rate actors, no one can wonder if it is utterly ineffective.

3. The real theatrical talent of the Germans was Kotzebue. . . . The second dramatic talent was Schiller.

4. The word tragedy is derived from the Greek word which means goat and the Greek word which means song. Tragedy is then, as it were, a goatish song—that is, foul like a goat.

5. The reason is perspicuous why no French plays, when translated, have succeeded or ever can succeed on the English stage.

6. Good music is a remedy against tediousness.

Cheap platitudes or—worse still—sheer ignorance, you chuckle. I am a complete and utter ass, you say. But hold a moment, and rest your blame. The first paragraph is by Schopenhauer. The second is by Goethe. The third is by Nietzsche. The fourth is by Dante. The fifth is by Dryden. And the sixth is the profound philosophy of Napoleon Bonaparte.

§ 115

Has anyone, in novel, short play, play or painting, ever failed completely who has taken the sea for his subject. It is the one theme that appears to resist not even the second-rate artist.

§ 116

It is my firm conviction, after due and protracted appraisal of all the rest of them, that the
average young American actress knows her job
better than any of her European rivals, save alone
the Austro-Hungarian. The American stage has
two talented young women for every one that the
French stage has, three for every one in England,
and at least a half dozen for every one in Germany.
This holds true not only of the dramatic stage,
but also of the musical comedy. Looking at the
Italian stage in five different years, I have seen
only two young women apparently under twenty-
five who were in any way the equal of any one of
three or four young women of the same age that
our stage reveals almost every season. With the
young men, however, it is a different, and ineffably
more grievous, story.

§ 117

Miss Marie Tempest is an admirable comedienne, a mistress of the thousand and one technical resources of polite comedy, an actress thoroughly schooled and extremely proficient in the arts
of light entertainment—who leaves one stone cold.
She belongs to that period of the theatre when an

actress was venerated in the degree that the means whereby she achieved her effects were superior to the effects achieved. While it may be true that the technique of the comedy stage has not changed at bottom, it is certainly true that the technique of the audiences of that stage has changed. And thus it comes about that the exceptionally experienced Miss Tempest is defeated by very reason of her exceptional experience. Her method is so sure that it misses. A comedienne with not one-half her talent, but with a measure and air of artlessness which she does not possess, today registers doubly in our theatre.

§ 118

To write a sound and interesting play with but three or four characters requires a measure of genius. The best that a playwright may otherwise contrive is a more or less conventional thing of the showshop with the conventional cast of nine or ten persons reduced to three or four by the laborious excision of the conventional butler, the maid, the family solicitor, the neighbour, his epigrammatic wife and pop-eyed daughter, and Uncle Farquhar from South Africa. The result is ever

less an authentic play of three or four characters
than a stereotyped theatre piece with a prudently
reduced salary list.

§ 119

The predestined heart and nature of the artist,
like those of every man, work obstinately—for all
his intense deliberation—in a great circle. They
come back eventually to the ingrafted point at
which they started; he cannot, however much he
tries to, change them, make them other than
generically they are, set them in other directions.
A Richard Strauss, for all his impudent and
fiery digressions, thus finds that he works
in a large circle from a "Serenade" to a "Rosen-
kavalier," a Flaubert from an "A Bord de la
Cange" to his reminiscences of Brittany, a Strindberg from a "Meister Olof" to an "Abu Casem's
Slippers" and a "Christmas," a Turgeniev from
his first poems to "Senilia," his last, a Veronese—
after a brave excursion into irony bordering upon blasphemy, as in "The Last Supper"—back
to the sentimental attitude toward theology as
illustrated in his "Coronation of the Virgin," a
Pinero from the syrups of a "Daisy's Escape,"
a "Bygones" and a "Sweet Lavender" to an "En-
chanted Cottage."

§ 120

Actors and boarding-school misses keep scrap-books.

§ 121

Anatole France speaks, in the same breath, with the candour of the Latin and the cunning of the Greek.

§ 122

The dirt of the bedroom farce . . . the sob stuff of the rural play . . . the tawdry melodrama of the 10-20-30 thriller . . . the sex alarums of the Broadway yokel-yanker . . . the bloody sensationalism of the Grand Guignol shocker . . . the nudity of the "Follies" . . . the extravagant murder and sudden death of the crook play . . . the dubious symbolism of the box-office neo-Maeterlincks . . . the bawdry of a Fourteenth Street burlesque show . . . the stretching of the long arm of coincidence as not even Theodore Kremer ever stretched it . . . the injection of propaganda gallery speeches . . . the banal eternal triangle hokum . . . In short, the greatest and most beautiful drama ever written. In short, the Bible.

PART II

THEATRE AND DRAMA

§ 1

The Immorality of French Drama.—The common assumption that the modern French drama is essentially an immoral drama, that it represents most greatly a departure from moral standard and purpose, is actually very far from true. There are, of course, examples in proof of their contention readily to be seized upon by the believers in the theory, but one cannot judge French drama by them any more than one can judge American drama by "A Bachelor's Night" or "The Demi-Virgin." For one such so-called immoral play as Guitry's "Veilleur de Nuit" or Coolus' "Mirette à Ses Raisons" or Valmonca's "Notre Femme et Cie" there are fifty such virginal plays as Guitry's "Pasteur," Verneuil's "Daniel" and Zamaçois' "Dame du Second." When one leaves the popular plays and ascends to a higher level, one finds the situation even more true. Nine-tenths of Donnay, Bataille, Hervieu, Capus, Lavedan, de Curel and, above all, Rostand, is fundamentally moral enough to satisfy even Mr. John S. Sumner. What play of these dramatists would Mr. Sumner even think

of suppressing on the ground of immorality? I
should like to hear its name. It is true, of course,
that there are certain things in certain boulevard
comedies and farces that, to the Anglo-Saxon
mind, are not au fait, but so do we find the same
sort of thing occasionally in our own Broadway
comedies and farces. I have seen or read most
of the Paris boulevard comedies and farces of
the last twenty years and in none of them have
I ever encountered dirtier lines than those in the
American "Getting Gertie's Garter" or a situation
more deliberately dirty than that in the second
act of the American "Please Get Married." The
rawest allusion in Guitry's "Wife, Husband and
Lover" pales into insignificance before a certain
allusion in Avery Hopwood's "Ladies' Night."
And the bed scene in "Le Sacrifice" has its match
in the American "Girl in the Limousine." The
so-called immoral popular drama of the later
years—comparatively speaking—is not the French,
but the German. (In the German, I include the
Austro-Hungarian.) The French playwright may
begin from what the Anglo-Saxon knows as an
immoral premise, but he generally ends upon
a moral conclusion. Not so the German. The
German playwright, and the Austro-Hungarian
with him, brings up where he begins. Catalogues
are tiresome; a few examples will suffice to sug-

gest a long train of others: Schnitzler and
"Reigen," Herczeg and "The Blue Fox," Rittner
and "En Route," Paul and "Tobacco Smoke,"
Misch and "The Little Prince," Schmidt and "Only
a Dream," Wedekind and "In Full Cry" (to say
nothing of a half dozen other longer plays, notably
"Pandora's Box"), Holm and "Mary's Big Heart,"
Jennings and "The Spanish Fly," together with
the plays of R. Göring, Max Pulver, Paul Korn-
feld, R. Lauchner, Földes, Georg Prinz, von
Schmitz, Frank and Geyer (who wrote "A Charming Person," played locally in expurgated form),
Lajos Biro, and, on occasion, Franz Molnar. For
every modern French play that seems to the Anglo-
Saxon critic to be immoral, one has no difficulty
in naming three German-Austro-Hungarian plays
that are equally, if not more, immoral. The
French drama, for all its detail of immorality,
is in its entirety a moral drama. Its wages of
sin is, pretty generally, death or marriage. For
one play by Pierre Veber that ends with a mistress,
there are a dozen by such dramatists as Capus that
end with a wife. For one play by de Caillavet
and de Flers that ends with wayward love trium-
phant, there are a dozen by such as Lavedan that
end with tragedy. And for one prefatorily immoral, but finally very moral, comedy like "The
Rubicon" of Edouard Bourdet, there are a dozen

like the consistently sentimental and proper "Silver Wedding" of Paul Géraldy.

§ 2

The Christ Play.—The intellectual and emotional maturity of a dramatist is to be determined by the age at which he writes his Christ play. Almost every writer for the theatre does a play about Christ some time in his life. Usually it is his first play, conceived while he is still in college and written either for the college literary paper or, soon after his graduation, for the Little Theatre of his home town. With such eternal undergraduates as Mr. Charles Rann Kennedy and the like, it comes much later in life, generally around the age of forty-eight or fifty. The Christ play seems to have a curious appeal to young men in their early twenties and old dramatic hacks. This is perhaps because, of all themes, the Christ theme is the easiest to handle. It is almost impossible to fail with it. The effect—registered for almost two thousand years—is ready-made for the playwright; the hush and thrill for which a writer with another theme has to sweat and struggle are here full-fledged and intact before he sets pen to paper. All that he has to do is to darken his stage, bring on a bad actor in a white nightshirt and coincidentally bring up the lights again—and the house is impressed as a score of Shaws and Synges could never impress it. Upon the printed page the Christ play makes no less an impression. Unlike any other piece of work, however bad it is, it wins attention and is promptly announced to be "reverent" or is violently denounced as in poor taste and blasphemous, the latter generally by the Jewish readers.

The Christ play usually follows one of four trends. In the first, the scene is a barn in Ohio whither come three men, the one a poet, the second a political economist, and the third a trombone player in a jazz cabaret. They enter the barn and find that an outcast woman has just had a a baby. The light from the single lantern in the barn casts a peculiar glow over the child. There is a strange silence about the place. The poet looks at the trombone player. With something of a tremour, he points to the child. "Do you know what night this is?" he asks the trombone player hoarsely. "Why—why—*it is Christmas Eve!*" responds the trombone player.

In the second version, the scene is a household of narrow, jealous, backbiting men and women. To the household comes a pale man dressed in an Inverness coat. He speaks pianissimo and when he learns that Delia, the servant girl, has been se-

duced by the jackanapes Hugo, defends her against
those who would cast her out into the stormy night.
This act exercises a profound influence on the
members of the household. "What is your name;
who are you?" they ask in hushed tones of the
stranger. "I am—" he begins. There is a peal
of thunder. "I am—" he begins again. There
is a flash of lightning. "I am—" he begins a
third time. There is a sound of church chimes.
The other characters look significantly from one
to another. There is a tense silence. The curtain falls.

In the third version, the figure of Christ does
not appear in the flesh. The scene is a gay wine
party on the outskirts of Jerusalem. The supers
are dressed like the Russian ballet; there is much
hoochie-coochie dancing; two Swobodas engage
in a wrestling match; an actress got up to look
like Theda Bara lies on a red couch at left with
an actor got up to look like Macbeth and kisses
him appassionato at frequent intervals, the while
two big coons from the "Shuffle Along" company
fan the twain with long palms; three of the union
musicians from the house orchestra who have been
sneaked up during the foregoing scene and have
been dressed like mandarins sit cross-legged on the
floor in a far corner and play the arghool, the
dremla and a kettle-drum; a fat actor supposed to

be very drunk lopes around the stage smirking lasciviously at the girls; someone periodically strikes a pair of cymbals; a large pot of Japanese punk burns at either side of the proscenium; a soubrette in strip tights with a tinseled diaper around her middle and a tin Sterno can on each of her breasts hotly embraces a tall actor made up to look like Marc Antony at the top of the flight of steps up-stage and, with their arms locked around each other, they roll down the stairs together; and a tenor from the old and defunct Wilbur Opera Co., dressed in yellow pajamas with green cuckoos embroidered on them, and representing a eunuch, passes drolly among the troupe with a tray of silver goblets. Suddenly there is a pause. The emotional actress, in the costume of Clytemnestra, enters slow-paced with bowed head. There is ribald mirth at her expense. She raises her head, looks long and straight at the critic for the *Staats-Zeitung*, and lifts her hand for silence. A queer look comes over the assemblage. "What is it? What is it, Obedildoch? What hast befallen thee, erst our queen of Love?" they bid. And, looking still long and straight at the critic for the *Staats*, and with a tri-facial neuralgic expression, the emotional actress breathes, "I have seen Him— the Nazarene!"

In the fourth version, there are either a couple

of old lions from the Sells-Floto circus or a
chariot race.

§ 3

On the Criticism of Laughter.—Looking back
over one's theatregoing years, one finds it somewhat irritating to one's critical pretensions to recall the considerable number of indifferent plays
that have given one excellent entertainment.
Surely one would have to work in the dramatic
department of the *Evening Post* to deny that, for
all their obvious critical imperfections, such things
as Guitry's farces, or Molnar's comedies, or Ar-
mont's, Dieudonné's and Schmidt's ironical
pastimes provide embarrassingly ingratiating diversion. It would, indeed, take a bravely uneducated man to contend seriously that a critically
exact play like Ibsen's "Master Builder" or Hauptmann's "Colleague Crampton" was half so entertaining in the theatre as some such dubious art
work as, say, "The School for Cocottes," or "The
Czarina," or "A Dressmaker's Apprentice Finds
A Position."

Nothing is more senseless and absurd than the
criticism of laughter. By laughter I do not, of
course, refer to the throat and intestinal violences
of stockbrokers, moving picture master-minds, stag

dinner party impresarios, Broadway geniuses and vulgarians of a stripe, but to the reaction of cultivated men and women. It is one of my critical beliefs—whether sound or not, I do not know, and care less—that anything that can make a cultured and intelligent man laugh has firm merit in it. Show me a play that can awaken the shades of laughter in such a man and I am prepared to argue any skeptic deaf, dumb and blind on the play's virtue, however much trouble I may have in assuaging certain of my critical doubts in the matter. If you tell me, in the midst of my argument, that I fail to discriminate between this kind of laughter and that, then I simply reply that any man who discriminates between two hearty laughs is idiotic enough to discriminate between two excellent brands of champagne because the labels are not identical. As I view the matter, Mr. George Bickel's fiddle tuning act is not less art of its sort than the most comical line in Beaumarchais. When criticism becomes snobbish it becomes imbecile. To say that Georges Feydeau's "On Purge Bébé" is not a good play but a very funny one is, though perhaps defensible on aesthetic grounds, akin to saying that Dempsey, though the world's champion, is not really a good pugilist. If a low and disreputable pun by George Robey succeeds in making some such man as

Arthur Schnitzler or Thomas Hardy or Anatole France or Arthur Balfour or General von Ludendorff laugh as much as the wittiest mot by Bernard Shaw, then I say that—since the sole object of both is the provoking of laughter—the pun is every bit as respectable as the other and more polished jest.

§ 4

Sex and Sentiment.—Sound and charming sentiment is impossible to a dramatist who does not constitutionally and philosophically view sex as either a humorous or a transient thing. The engaging full-bodied sentiment of humorous sex distilled by such writers as de Caillavet and de Flers and the equally engaging and equally full-bodied sentiment of transitory sex distilled by such as Arthur Schnitzler persistently evade the playwright who sees sex otherwise. It is paradoxical but true, indeed, that a dramatist generically sentimental is rarely able to write winning sentiment—the only exception that comes to mind at the moment being Barrie. The general American playwright thus labours under a double handicap in that, being an American, he is a sentimentalist by nature and in that, being a sentimentalist by nature, he is able to conceive of sex in but one of two ways: either as a Sunday School, or as the third act of "King Lear." That is to say, he is brought to view sex either as something sweet and sacred, or as something dramatic and stormful. The result is a drama wherein the sex organs are located, in the first instance, two inches to the left in the upper portion of the thorax or, in the second, in the bronchial tubes and caruncula lacrymalis. In this the American playwright betrays himself particularly when he essays the business of adapting the plays of dramatists constituted differently from himself. Their words, their situations, the externals of their characters he is able to translate, but their philosophies, their emotions, their charm and humour, he is unable to adapt. He is unable to do this for the same reason that a Frenchman is unable to look right in a derby hat, or that a Viennese is unable to drink rye whisky, or that an Italian is unable to sing a ragtime song. These things are alien to him and, whatever his affectation and pretence, they do not fit him or suit him.

§ 5

The Charm of Bad Acting.—Sitting before the performances of Mr. William Gillette in such concoctions of arch nonsense as "The Dream Maker," one is reminded again of the great charm that so often reposes in what is, critically, bad acting. This Gillette, by any sound standard, is a mere trickster of acting; it is perhaps not too much to say that, as an actor, he is to his craft what O. Henry was to his; yet there are surely few to deny that, for all his low estate as an histrionic artist, he is one of the most thoroughly watchable and engaging performers on our stage. And what is the secret of the paradox? The secret, very simply, is that bad acting often enchants by virtue of its very artlessness, where highly proficient acting leaves one cold. Acting that lacks sound artistic design is, in this, much like some ugly old easy chair. It has much of the cozy warmth, comfortableness, ease and agreeable friendliness that a beautiful, stiff Sheraton lacks.

If acting is an art at all, it is the baby art. And, like a baby, sophistication is, or should be, relevantly a stranger to it. Acting that is polished to the last degree is like a butler—distinguishedly lifeless. Mankind is itself a bad and fitful actor. Imitations of mankind upon the stage should have all of mankind's flaws, weaknesses, crudities and mistakes. Gillette commits a hundred sins against histrionic art in every one of his performances. Walter Hampden, to take a single example, commits not a tenth that number. Yet Gillette is ten times as pleasant an actor to watch. He is as

charming in his imperfections as the dancing of a
little girl of six. His monotonous voice has thrice
the captivating quality of the fluid voice of a dozen
Russ Whytals; his single awkward gesture six
times the eloquence of the studied gestures of all
the John Masons who ever tortured the public eye.

Gillette, however, is not the only bad actor
whose very badness is refractorily fascinating.
Cyril Keightly is another; Eric Maturin (whom
we haven't laid eyes on since "Mid-Channel") is
another; and Reginald Barlow is still another.
Dismiss from your thought, please, any notion that
what I am writing here is an attempt at left-handed
smartness. I mean seriously that these men are
exceptionally effective actors because of their artistic guilt rather than in spite of it. They are,
from the standpoint of penetrating criticism, not
ranking actors, but they are actors who get illusion
out of one as colleagues twice as proficient cannot.
Where an artistically cruder actor than Lowell
Sherman; yet where, in certain rôles, one more
peculiarly productive of results? Or, again, take
such performers as Charles Cherry, Harry Mest-
ayer, John Miltern, Kenneth Douglas, John West-
ley, James Rennie and Frank Sheridan. Surely
it would be a school-boy of a critic who would be
so rash as to say that any of these are first-rate actors or—some of them—even second-rate actors.

Yet surely it would be an old fogy of a critic who would not be so rash as to admit that they very often are doubly as effective as actors of vastly greater finish and position.

Just as there is sometimes in a performance of amateurs a winning quality that one does not find in a performance of professionals, so is there sometimes in a crude professional performance a winning quality that one does not find in a suave professional performance. To quote the hoary byword: It may not be art, but it's life. Our tastes and prejudices are stubbornly built that way. We —or at least those of us who are not given overly to critical affectation—have to admit that lack of sound merit is occasionally even more beguiling than sound merit. A perfectly rudimentary and untutored acting performance like that of little Miss Faire Binney in such an exhibition of trash as "The Teaser" thus proves twice as refreshing as would the performance of another actress of twice Miss Binney's technical skill. Again, such a performance as that of Frank Shannon, in "Anna Christie," certainly one full of technical flaws, proves twice as felicitous as would one by an actor like Brandon Tynan who is possessed of a greatly superior technical equipment. The positive charm of bad acting may readily be detected in the instance of such a performance as is often given by the veteran, William H. Thompson. There is to this actor's bad acting a quality paradoxically so fetching and altogether captivating that he dominates the stage even on such occasions as it is simultaneously occupied by actors much better than himself. This phenomenon is often ascribed idiotically to what is termed personality. But personality, in the sense that the word is thus used, has—unless I am very much in error—little or nothing to do with the case. I have seen Thompson on a stage with actors admitted to have personalities double the voltage of his own (and possessed of double his technical resource), yet the old fellow has promptly won away from them the eye and ear and heart of his audience.

Personality is a word employed by critics to conceal their failure to penetrate certain evasive paradoxes of acting. Surely Lou Tellegen has personality, but does it ever avail him anything when he is on the stage, whether in a company of good actors or bad? Emmett Corrigan has personality and so has Robert Warwick, and what does it profit them? No, the charm that often inheres in bad acting has very little to do with the personality of the actor. Take, for example, the case of John Flood. Flood has scarcely any of this so-called personality; he is a bad actor; yet he is more effective nine times in ten than any other actor with personality and sound histrionic ability would be in the same rôles. The same thing holds true of such actors as Joseph Kilgour and, one might even go so far as to say, Fritz Williams.

Acting, in good truth, is a chameleon ever beset by the intricate plaids of its spectators' tastes, idiosyncrasies and temperaments. Its colours change constantly, even though its fundamental shade may be blue—very. If fifty thousand people consider Robert B. Mantell the greatest Shakespearian actor who was ever born in Ayrshire, Scotland, on February 7, 1854, fifty thousand others consider him the worst. And if, on the other hand, one hundred thousand persons think that Duse is the greatest actress of our time, there are a great many who think her nothing of the sort. Acting always rebelliously reminds me of ham and cabbage: you like it if it agrees with you, and don't like it if it doesn't—and it is comparatively just as much art. Personally, give me William Gillette, the bad actor, and you may have all the good actors like Pedro de Cordoba that you can lay your hands on. I once wrote of E. W. Howe that his peculiar agreeableness as a surveyor of the human comedy lay in the fact that he possessed all the virtues and all the defects of one's own father. The peculiar agreeableness of such an actor as Gillette perhaps lies in the fact that he acts publicly with all the artistic crudity that the rest of us act privately.

§ 6

The Press and the Drama.—An attempt to decipher the precise standpoint from which the gentlemen on the New York newspapers criticize the drama presents a rich perplexity. It is commonly, and often correctly, believed that the newspaper reviewer is instructed to criticize the drama from the standpoint of that vague soul known now as the average man and now as the man in the street; but a study of the New York critical compositions leads one to doubt that, if this is the case, the reviewing gentlemen are obeying orders. For surely the average man or the man in the street regards "East Is West" and "The Man Who Came Back" and even "Bluebeard's Eighth Wife" with all the enthusiasm that the journalistic reviewer fails to. But if the newspaper reviewer does not view drama with the eyes of the average man, does he view it with the eyes of the sophisticated and cultured man? Again one studies his compositions, and again one is baffled. For if he viewed drama from this more reserved and civilized seat he could not possibly see the virtues in such inferior plays as "The Detour" and "Daddy's Gone A-Hunting" that he fails to see in such work as "Papa" and "The Gentile Wife" and, above all, in "The Children's Tragedy." Well, then, if he does not take either of these positions in his surveys, what position does he take? It is commonly believed that he appraises drama with the mind of the simon-pure, undiluted numskull, but—though one is sometimes sorely tempted by the facts in such instances as "Swords" to believe it—one finds that this also is not the case. For, if it were, he would succumb to such things as "Tarzan of the Apes" and "Oh Marion" in a fashion that he happily does not. But if he does not criticize drama as an average man, or as a cultured man, or as a complete mooncalf, as what does he criticize it? Contrary to my customary and often highly irritating practice of having a facile solution for everything under the sun, I give it up.

But though I am unable to solve the rebus, I privilege myself a guess or two. The newspaper reviewer, as I inspect him, strikes me as viewing drama with the blanket journalistic eye of his managing editor. This latter eye is one excessively practical yet excessively eager not to seem too practical: a mixture of commerce and timorous, prudent idealism. And the reviewer feels the glare of this managing editorial eye, however thick the wall that separates the two offices. The typical New York managing editor is a suave and eely fellow profoundly gifted with a talent for sitting simultaneously on the cashier and art supplement stools without falling between them. On one and the same page he can—or at least hopes and prays he can—tickle Bishop Manning, Henry Cabot Lodge, Julius Rosenwald, Johann Sebastian Bach, Valeska Suratt, General Foch, Lloyd George, the Japs, Rodin, and Stern Brothers. And in order to mask his encompassing and prosperous conciliatory nature, and by way of not letting all the cat out of the bag, he occasionally fetches up a few alibis for himself in the obscure persons of a Yiddish sweatshop operator whose doors are found to have been bolted when the fire broke out, George Sylvester Viereck, Butler Davenport, John Roach Straton, or some Third Avenue manufacturer of evil frankfurters.

The successful newspaper, the managing editor appreciates, must please a preponderant majority of its readers and this preponderant majority, he also fully appreciates, is of the stout belief that art, while commendable in a dubious way and even perhaps not entirely reprehensible (like the exploits of an heroic German ace, for example), is yet a poor witness for the defence. In order to get this majority to swallow dramatic art at all, it is necesary, he knows, to coat it with a deceptive critical sugar coating made up of allusions to spaghetti, quotations from Rudyard Kipling's worst poems, references to the A. E. F. and the long cigars that John Stetson used to smoke, jokes about the suit worn by the juvenile, bad puns, and observations to the effect that the child (phonetically spelled) is in the British capital. The play reviewer presently catches this critical measles and remains permanently ill with the ailment; and as time goes on his compositions become progressively more measles and less criticism. The result is a contemplation of drama that is infinitely less a contemplation of drama as art than a sedulous and ingenious avoidance of contemplation of drama as art—in other words, a straddling of the question. A glance at almost any New York newspaper for a week running will indicate clearly to what extent this straddling goes. Drama is criticized in terms of the Algonquin Hotel, the Polo Grounds, the Actors' Equity Ball or, by the older fellows, in terms of the United Missionaries Society, the free lunch that used to be served in Augustin Daly's greenroom, or Madame Janauschek's emotional equipment, but never in terms of æsthetics. The only time drama is ever considered in the newspapers as an art is when something is produced in the Neighbourhood Playhouse down in Grand street, which is far enough away not to bother anyone.

But as a general rule the view, in the old phrase, is of "the drama and other sports."

In the case of the plays of Eugene O'Neill, for instance, one gets a particularly clear idea of the manner in which this metropolitan journalistic criticism cavorts. Surely if any playwright in America deserves, or has ever deserved, to be considered as a dignified artist, it must be agreed that O'Neill is that man. Yet, save in two cases, he is regularly treated not as an artist-dramatist but exactly as if he were a mere box-office jobber like Max Marcin or Cosmo Hamilton, and his plays not as works of artistic merit or demerit but as so many vaudeville jugglers or trained dogs. He is subjected not to the standards of æsthetics, but to those of popular drama. He is criticized not as a sincere and honest writer, whether good or bad, but as a fabricator of showshop stuffs. They deplore that, unlike the vastly more agreeable and sunshiny Winchell Smith and Edward Childs Carpenter, he seems to see human life chiefly as an inscrutable and gloomy piece of irony on the part of the gods—like Joseph Conrad and Fédor Dostoievski. They lament that his themes (unlike George V. Hobart's) are drab and sordid—like Zola's and Andreyev's. They deny (and offer the works of Augustus Thomas in proof) that life as O'Neill pictures it is just that way. And when, as in the case of "Anna Christie," he does not see life "that way," but sees it with a touch of rainbow athwart its skies, they recall his past work and snicker self-satisfiedly that he has arbitrarily stuck a theatrical happy ending onto his play. In them the poison of the show-shop has worked so long that it is simply impossible for them to consider him as an autonomous artist and not as a theatrical offspring of some couple like Eugene Walter and Rida Johnson Young. And when they bravely seek to save their faces by straddling the question, the result is no less opéra bouffe. Criticism may straddle nothing. Positive or not positive, certain or doubtful, enthusiastic or disgusted, it must lead by the head or pull by the tail. The American journalistic criticism has in the main absurdly tried to handle O'Neill by sitting half in the saddle and half in the buggy.

§ 7

The Biographical Play.—Of all plays, the so-called biographical one is undoubtedly the easiest to write. Consider, in example, the following scene from a famous play:

Enter Jean Jacques Rousseau.

Rousseau—I am deeply grieved, Madame—(*he recog-*

nizes Thérèse Le Vasseur with a start). Mon Dieu! You, Thérèse—here!

Thérèse—Ah, Jean Jacques, I could not die until I had your forgiveness. Do not turn away from me—bear with me one small moment—only say that you will forgive me, and I can rest in peace.

Rousseau—Why did you come here?

Thérèse—I could not stay away from you and my children. The longing for the sight of them was killing me. I knew no moment's peace after the mad act I was guilty of—in leaving you. Not an hour had I departed ere repentance set in. Even then I would have come back, but I did not know how. My sin was great, and my punishment has been greater; it has been one long, long mental agony.

Rousseau—Why did you go away?

Thérèse—Did you not know why?

Rousseau—No; it was ever a mystery to me.

Thérèse—I went out of love for you. Ah, do not look at me in that reproachful way! I loved you dearly, and I grew to doubt you. I thought you false and deceitful to me; that your love was given to another, and, in my sore jealousy, I listened to the temptings of the man who whispered of revenge. But it was not so—tell me it was not so, Jean!

Rousseau—Can you ask me that, knowing me as you did then, and as you must have known me since? I was not false to you in word, in thought, or in deed, Thérèse.

Thérèse—I know it now, mon cher, but I was mad. I could not have committed the act save in madness. Say, mon Jean Jacques, that you will forget all and forgive me!

Rousseau— I cannot forget—I have forgiven already.

You recognize it immediately, if a bit vaguely. One of the greatest successes the theatre has ever known. But you cannot recall its title? I supply it: "East Lynne." I have quoted the old lulu word for word and have merely re-named Archibald Carlyle Jean Jacques Rousseau and Lady Isabel Thérèse Le Vasseur. The dialogue fits the lives of Rousseau and his mistress-wife quite as snugly and accurately as is the general case in biographical plays. And the same thing may be done just as simply, effectively and no doubt as profitably, with "The Lady of Lyons" by calling Claude Melnotte Verlaine, with "Camille" by calling Marguerite Gautier Madame Rachel and renaming Armand after one of her more persistent and devoted lovers, and with "Up in Mabel's Room" by naming the central male character King Edward VII, late Prince of Wales.

§ 8

Handicap.—It is the critical custom regularly to herald Mr. Winthrop Ames as a theatrical producer of exceptional taste simply because he is known to be a gentleman whose family occupies a position of considerable social importance in the fashionable Back Bay section of Boston. The fact that Mr. Ames is actually a theatrical pro-

ducer of exceptional taste is a contradiction of
his birth and social position rather than a predi-
cate. Two of the theatrical directors whose exceptional taste has placed them today in the front
rank of the world's producers are, respectively,
the son of a drunken hooligan and the son of a
cheap actor. The beauty of the theatre at its
highest and finest usually comes out of the gutter.
Mr. Ames has surmounted his handicap splen-
didly. It must have been a tough fight. His
excellent productions of the various plays he has
sponsored, tactful, tasteful and at times theatrically brilliant, have been worthy of the son of
a poor pushcart peddler.

§ 9

Our Leading Shakespearian Actor.—Though
John Barrymore's admirable Richard and Faversham's no less admirable Iago are not out of
memory, Mr. Fritz Leiber's consistently fine work
in a comprehensive repertoire gives him, I believe,
the leadership of our Shakespearian stage. Beside this Leiber, Mantell takes on the aspect of a
bull attempting to play the zither, Hampden of
a college professor dancing to a gipsy tune, and
Sothern of a distinguished New England grandpa dressed up as Romeo at a fancy ball. Hackett,

of course, is nowhere: Shakespeare is far beyond
his talent. In Leiber there is all the born sense
of poetry and drama and wild, passionate beauty
that these others lack. Without the force of presence possessed by certain of the others, he is able,
out of his voice and features, out of his emotional
equipment and body swing, to send the blood of
grandeur shooting afresh through the text of the
great poet. They say he is intelligent, and hence
the fine actor that he is. Bosh. He is merely
obedient. He has the sound sense to read the
simple and wonderful line not like an actor who
would be a savant but like an actor who would be
merely an actor. Hence his great eloquence.
Leiber knows more about *acting* Shakespeare than
all the other American actors who concern themselves chiefly with *understanding* him. He is,
first and foremost, a player. To his colleagues he
is content to leave all the extrinsic nonsenses—all
the psycho-analyzings of character, all the
"theories" of interpretation, and all the diagnoses
of intent—of which they are so grotesquely fond.

§ 10

Hamlet Sans Hamlet.—The classics and most
of first-rate modern drama aside, it remains that
three-quarters of the rest of the drama of today

would be measurably improved were its central
rôles omitted.   These central rôles, where they
have not been manufactured merely to satisfy the
vanities of star actors, represent generally the
fatuous ratiocinations and philosophies of skilful
playwrights who are otherwise ignorant men.
And the omission of them, accordingly, would
not only enhance the purely dramatic value of
the plays, but the intellectual quality no less.
Omit the nonsensical propaganda impersonated by
the leading rôles in two out of three of Brieux's
plays, and what remains is lively and intelligent
theatre drama.   Delete the sophomoric animad-
versions that take human form in the star rôles
of three out of four of Augustus Thomas' plays,
and what remains is workmanlike and interesting
theatrical entertainment.

The star rôle in the majority of modern plays
is more often than not designed to be a mirror of
the mob's thoughts, ideas, ambitions and admirations.   To omit it would be to inform these plays
with a greater degree of sophistication and culture.
Consider, in example, how greatly such plays as
those of the average actor-manager's would be
improved were the star rôles with their empty
heroisms, sentimentalisms and homilies left out.
Consider, in further example, how much sounder
such a play as "The Witching Hour" would be

were the rôle of Justice Prentice with its absurd
speeches like "Margaret Price—people will say
that she has been in her grave thirty years, but
I'll swear her spirit was in this room tonight and
directed a decision of the Supreme Court of the
United States!" blue-penciled. And this, for all
the circumstance that the remaining rôle of Jack
Brookfield, with its not less idiotic, "I've put
people practically asleep in a chair and I've made
them tell me what a boy was doing, a mile away,
in a jail," is, in the tournament of bosh, actually
the star actor rôle.

Speaking more accurately with the above in
mind, it is perhaps the so-called "attorney" rôles
in the majority of modern plays rather than the
star actors' rôles that were best omitted, though
the two are often identical. These "attorney"
rôles represent more exactly the mob audience's
point of view. But, leaving aside a splitting of
hairs, the conviction persists that such plays as
Macdonald Hastings' "The New Sin" would be as
greatly bettered were the rôle of Hilary Cutts—
with its philosophy that "people enjoy being miserable, but they never dare admit anything of the
sort"—stricken out as would be such plays as
Rachel Crothers' "He and She" were the rôle of
the wife, Ann Herford, with its philosophy that

"the more a woman knows, the more she has to give to her children and to the home."

§ 11

The Motion Pictures.—The champions of the motion picture, replying to the doubters, urge that the cinema is still in its infancy and that it is therefore unjust to compare it with the other arts. "Give the motion pictures time," they cry. "Think of the other arts in *their* infancy!" Fair enough, gentlemen. Think of the drama in its infancy. Think of sculpture in its infancy. Think of architecture in its infancy. Think of literature in its infancy. And, gentlemen, keep on thinking!

§ 12

Plausibility and the Theatre.—No mystery play, provided only it be manufactured with a fair amount of skill, can be too absurd for the popular palate. "The Cat and the Canary," a straight melodrama, was not less incredible than "Officer 666," a melodramatic farce; and yet it was equally successful. The notion that the public will watch with close attention a melodramatic farce like the latter simply because it is admitted

to be a farce, but will not watch with the same
close nervous attention a somewhat straighter
melodrama like "The Bat," because it is not announced as an out-and-out farce, is something
like the notion that the public would not have
been thrilled as much as it actually was by a play
like "Arséne Lupin" if that play had been designated a farce (which it was) instead of a straight
melodrama (which, despite the designation, it assuredly was not). The incredible melodrama
generally makes very much more money in the
theatre than the more reasonable melodrama.
"Within the Law," an enormous money-maker, was
completely without conviction in its three biggest
scenes. Not even the mind of a policeman could
have been bamboozled by them. "The Thir-
teenth Chair," another success, was absurdity even
to a moron, yet consistently holding. Such considerably more plausible melodramas as "The
Knife" and "The Assassin" of Eugene Walter, on
the other hand, were failures. And this despite
the fact that they were more dexterous pieces of
dramatic writing than either of the other melodramas. The theory that the theatre must be
plausible to pay is the theory that plausibility is
inevitably a better circus than a boozy and asinine
fancy.

§ 13

J. M. Barrie.—The genial Professor William Lyon Phelps, Yale's literary Heffelfinger and champion intercollegiate endorser, now turns from his Monday endorsement of Blasco Ibáñez, Johan Bojer and Sanatogen, his Tuesday endorsement of Maeterlinck, Edith M. Hull and Pompeiian Massage Cream, and his Wednesday matinée endorsement of Rose Macauley, Maxwell Bodenheim and Porosknit Undershirts, to J. M. Barrie. "Barrie," proclaims the Professor, who in his comprehensive catalogue of testimonials has included even the somewhat over-rated George Jean Nathan, "is the foremost English-writing dramatist of our time, and his plays, taken together, make the most important contributions to the English drama since Sheridan.   He unites the chief qualities of his contemporaries, and yet the last word to describe his work would be the word eclectic.   For he is the most original of them all.   He has the intellectual grasp of Galsworthy, the moral earnestness of Jones, the ironical mirth of Synge, the unearthly fantasy of Dunsany, the consistent logic of Ervine, the wit of Shaw, the technical excellence of Pinero. And in addition to these qualities, he has a combination of charm and tenderness possessed by no

other man." Which, rolling an eye back over the
Professor's grand total of 127,862 endorsements
since March 1, 1917, may be said to be a trifle
more fulsome than even his testimonials in behalf
of Henry Van Dyke, Cyrus Townsend Brady, Ro-
dolph Valentino and the Gem Safety Razor.

This marshaling of Barrie's multiple and stupendous geniuses appears in an essay the introduction
to which reads as follows: "Perhaps the most intelligent attitude to take toward the plays of J. M.
Barrie is unconditional surrender. If one unreservedly yields one's mind and heart to their enfolding
charm, then one will understand them." An introduction typical of most of the critical hypotheses
and appraisals of Barrie and which, alas, cruelly
betrays such violent partisans as the amiable Professor. The paradox of "intelligent attitude" and
"unreserved yielding of one's mind" tells the story:
a logic quite as dapper as that which would maintain that the most intelligent attitude to take toward
the novels of Hall Caine is one of unconditional
surrender. For it is plain that if one unreservedly
yields one's intelligence to the novels of the Manx
Robert Keable, as the Professor bids one do in the
instance of the plays of Barrie, these novels may
also seem the most important contributions to English literature since Thackeray.

Most of the criticism of Barrie pursues this blind

and amorous manner.   Barrie is not criticized; he
is caressed.   He is viewed not as a subject for
deliberate analysis and appraisement, as all other
dramatists are viewed, but much in the spirit of
"Home, Sweet Home," the Declaration of Independence, Edith Cavell, and Mother.   He is the belle
amie, the inamorata, of modern Anglo-Saxon
dramatic criticism, the Florence Nightingale of the
modern Anglo-Saxon theatre.   Arguments that are
in specific instances used against other dramatists
are in the selfsame instances lavishly employed in
his favour.   Thus, Chesterton's "Magic" is criticized for the very qualities for which Barrie's
"Peter Pan" is eulogized, Strindberg's "Dream
Play" for the same technical qualities for which
Barrie's "A Kiss for Cinderella" is praised, and
Arnold Bennett's "Milestones" for the long lapses
of time, allegedly inimical to the dramatic unities,
for which Barrie's "Mary Rose" is applauded.
The detached intellectual point of view of Galsworthy and the moral earnestness of Jones, regarded in each instance as somewhat damaging to
the best effect of the plays of these dramatists, suddenly, when attributed to Barrie, become
assets.   Shaw is severely criticized for taking far
fewer technical liberties with his medium than Barrie has taken; the latter has, more than any other
modern English-speaking dramatist, disregarded

the accepted rules of dramatic composition; "Peter Pan" and "Mary Rose" are to Shaw's technique what Georg Kaiser's "Morning Until Midnight" is to Pinero's "Preserving Mr. Panmure." "A Kiss for Cinderella," written by any one other than Barrie, would have been snickered off the stage. And the same with "Mary Rose."

It is the commonest claim in behalf of Barrie's pre-eminence that his plays "because of his imagination that has played on the things which are common to all men in all ages," will outlive those of such a dramatist as, say, Shaw in the repertoire of the English-speaking theatre. It might similarly, and with the same measure of truth, be claimed in behalf of the pre-eminence of Mrs. Henry Wood that, because her imagination played on the things which are common to all men in all ages, her "East Lynne" has outlived in the repertoire of the English-speaking theatre the plays of such contemporaries as, say, the translated Meilhac, Labiche and Barrière. Or that the greater endurance of "La Dame aux Camélias" makes "La Dame aux Camélias" a finer play than "Les Faux Bonshommes" or "Le Voyage de M. Perrichon" which were produced at about the same time. Endurance and quality are not always bed-fellows. "Charley's Aunt" has outlived three-quarters of the better plays of the era of its birth, and "Uncle

Tom's Cabin" will doubtless outlive all the American plays (save perhaps such kindred masterpieces as "Ben Hur" and "Way Down East") written since Harriet Beecher Stowe's day. That one or two of Barrie's plays will endure is very likely. But these plays, notably "Peter Pan," will endure not as, say, "Le Misanthrope" has endured, but as "Little Red Riding Hood" or "Jack the Giant Killer." Or, in another way of putting it, as the worst fairy tale of the Grimms will outlive the best realistic tale of Hermann Sudermann. The question is not one strictly of art and quality, but of psychic soothing power and universal applicability. Just so has the mustard plaster outlived Népomucène Lemercier's "Pinto."

The Barrie dervishes permit nothing to stand in the way of their canonization; they drag up artillery from the most bizarre quarters and fire indiscriminately to the right and left. Not to succumb wholeheartedly to Barrie is, in their decision, akin to standing out against daily bathing and the Monroe Doctrine. A vulgar and anti-social theatrical act, much like keeping one's hat on when the curtain goes up or talking during a death scene. The peculiar nature of the pro-Barrie artillery finds illustration in such jocosities as the New York _Times_' recent critical contrasting of Barrie and Shaw wherein the latter was peremptorily disposed of with the remark, "Shaw, while he has gradually been able to gather about him a sufficiently large public that understand his idiom, has never persuaded any other playwrights to use it," the *Times* presumably not being privy to the names of such playwrights as Granville Barker, Wedekind, MacDonald Hastings, Schnitzler (in "Professor Bernhardi") Otto Soyka, H. Müller, Brieux, Felix Salten, Leo Birinski, Lennox Robinson (in "Patriots"), Freksa, the Rubinstein who wrote "Consequences," Gabriel Trarieux, and the Americans Tom Barry (in "The Upstart," that regrettably slighted play) and Lawrence Langner (in "The Family Exit")—to say nothing of hundreds of hopeful amateurs the world over. And in supplementary illustration, to return to our Yale friend, the bomb: "For sheer audacity, it would be difficult to parallel the opening of 'What Every Woman Knows.' The curtain rises and not a word is spoken for seven minutes. To conceive and insist on such a situation is an indication of how much confidence the playwright had in himself, and in his audience. His confidence was justified, though it would be foolhardy for another to imitate it." Although it may come as something of a shock to the good Phelps, the fact remains— unless my memory betrays me—that he may in this paragraph substitute for "What Every Woman Knows" a play called "Broadway Jones," and for Barrie the name of George M. Cohan.

I suppose that no man has had more enjoyment from certain of Barrie's plays than I have had. I have seen "'Peter Pan" a half dozen times, and shall doubtless see it a half dozen times more. "The Admirable Crichton," "Alice-Sit-by-the Fire," "The Legend of Leonora," "The Twelve Pound Look," these and yet others have constituted pleasant evenings in the theatre for me. Good plays, all; but first-rate plays? Hardly. Of them all "Peter Pan" perhaps comes closest to the high level. The rest, at their best, are meritorious second-raters; at their worst—the worst of "Mary Rose," for instance,—eighth-rate flubdub. If Shaw's trick is a statement of the obvious in terms of the scandalous, Barrie's may be described as a statement of the sentimental is terms of the mildly cynical. This is a shrewd trick, and one that never, or rarely ever, fails in the theatre. It is also a trick that rarely fails to hypnotize the critics. Holding out against the purely sentimental by way of proving themselves so many coldly reasoning Nietzsches, they are duped by the screen of mild cynicism and brought to terms. And, thus duped, they mistake the agreeable and soothing evening spent in the theatre for a sure sign of genius behind the footlights. . . . Barrie is a sort of

effeminate Schnitzler. Both frequently work in
much the same fundamental manner; but where
Schnitzler, a fine artist, stands above his marionettes and out of his catholic understanding of human frailties resolutely manipulates the strings
that control them, Barrie, merely a fine artisan,
too often confuses himself with his marionettes,
mingles amongst them and becomes tangled up in
the wires. The criticism of Shaw and Wilde,
that every character in a Shaw or Wilde play talks
like Shaw or Wilde, applies as well to Barrie.
Barrie, however, cleverly deceives his critics in
this regard by the simple device of utilizing the
Hanlon Brothers' "Fantasma" scenery and technique, or by the equally simple device, as in "The
Admirable Crichton," of playing Shaw and Wilde
without chairs. The scenery moves; the lights do
fancy tricks; the actors, instead of quietly sitting
down and making epigrams, crack their whimsies
while suspended on wires in mid-air; and the on-
looking critics, bedazzled by the excitement of
the hocus-pocus, fail to observe that their beloved
one is doing the precise thing that they loudly condemned in Wilde and still loudly condemn in
Shaw.

Barrie, in short, is a very agreeable playwright
whose personal weaknesses, being common to
many of his critics, are subconsciously converted

by these critics into virtues. Their own sentimentality is echoed in his, and their own protective colouration of assumed cynicism is reflected in his. It is not Barrie whom they admire so much as it is themselves. Where a dramatist like Shaw is on to them, and cruelly gives them away, Barrie, being one of them and like them, protects them and amiably keeps their secret. A gentleman . . . an excellent showman . . . an often winning and skilful playwright . . . a second-rate genius.

"Mary Rose" marks the climax of the Scotch Maeterlinck's disintegration, the first unmistakable symptoms of which were detected some eight or nine years ago and thereafter showed a successive positive reaction in "A Kiss for Cinderella," "Old Friends," "Rosy Rapture," "The Truth About the Russian Dancers," and "Dear Brutus." This "Mary Rose," indeed, is Barrie unconsciously travestying Barrie: the Barrie technique suffering from auto-intoxication. All the much lauded Barrie qualities, the old "charm," "wistfulness," "eerie fancy" and "delicate imagination," are here assembled and raised to the nth. The "charm" is laid on with a shovel; the "wistfulness" and "eerie fancy" are poured in with a fire hose; and the general proceedings are imaginative to the point of inanity, as, for example, when the world-battered soldier son takes the ghost of his mother on his lap, fondles her and addresses her as "ghostie." The basic idea of the play (to Professor Phelps' mind doubtless suggestive of the intellectual grasp of Galsworthy) rests in the profoundly philosophical thesis that love does not last forever. This thesis Barrie has developed crazy-quilt fashion in a play that is so exaggeratedly fanciful as to be almost inarticulate. It is as if Barrie had succumbed to the Expressionism species of dramaturgy and had sought to practise the form without having assimilated its principles. I venture to say that were the play transferred from the stage of such a theatre as the Empire to the Winter Garden, cast with Winter Garden mimes and played perfectly straight and literally, any person who had not seen it before would vote it a searching and extremely jocose burlesque of Barrie. The impression one gets from the play is of watching Prof. Mysto, the hypnotist, astound the country-jakes by making the local grocery boy (bribed with a dollar to act as a "plant") believe that he is an angel. It is silly stuff; it explodes a considerable portion of the Barrie balloon that critics these many years have been assiduously and rapturously inflating; it brings one to turn again to a closer scrutiny of its author's antecedent plays that one has admired, and to ponder . . . and to ponder . . .

§ 14

Adultery in Falseface.—Outright adultery in
the farce, as the French employ it, would, I believe, be not nearly so objectionable to American
morals as the euphemistic substitutes and sexual
false-faces currently in vogue. For all the circumstance that such a French farce as, say, Gan-
dera's "Le Coucher de la Mariée" or Veber's
"Mon Amour Cheri" deals frankly with adultery,
it would be less discommodious to the moral sense
of an American audience than such farces as Avery
Hopwood writes, since a moral sense of the species
that we encounter locally is ever offended less by
literary saltpetre than by literary cantharides.
Against which type of novel, for example, do the
professional moralists most often bend their en-
ergies: the novel of consummated adultery or the
novel of cunningly deferred adultery? Against
which type of play, further, do they direct their
efforts: the play of outright adultery, like "Iris"
or "The Claw" or "Hindle Wakes," or the play of
craftily presaged but sedulously side-stepped adultery, like "The Girl with the Whooping Cough"
or "Pretty Soft" or "The Demi-Virgin?" It was
not the adultery that set the moralists upon Cabell's
"Jurgen," but the double entente. It was not the

adultery that set them upon Dreiser's "The 'Genius,'" but the episodes leading up to the adultery.

§ 15

The Test of the Comedian.—There are many comedians who appropriately—if disastrously—resemble a good joke. They are very funny the first time you hear them, and very flat the second. Whatever the nature of the material with which they may be equipped, they lack the comic ectoplasm that on this second occasion distinguishes the true comic spirit from the false. Any person who has gone to the theatre regularly for a period of years will easily recall any number of comedians who have impressed him as exceptionally ludicrous fellows the first time he saw them and who the next time impressed him as being every bit as jolly as a thesis on Obrenovitch Milosh and the second Serbian war of liberation. To how many of you was Eddie Foy comic after the first time? Or Frank Daniels? Or Frank Moulan? Or Fred Frear? Or Harry Bulger? Or Lawrance D'Orsay, or John E. Henshaw, or Arthur Dunn, or Herbert Corthell, or Ralph Herz, or Jefferson De Angelis, or Dallas Welford, or Victor Moore, or Ned Sparks, or Harry Fisher? Or any one of a dozen others?

The test of a real comedian rests in whether
you laugh at him before he opens his mouth.
After he opens his mouth any comedian, first-class
or tenth-class, may be moderately comic if only
the ex-soft-shoe-dancer who supplies him with lines
be comic; but the true comedian would be a comedian still were he suddenly to be stricken with
lockjaw, and with tonsilitis, mumps and quinsy as
complications. There is something about a first-
class comedian that is always just a little more
comic than the most comical line he speaks or the
most comical song he sings. And it isn't his nose,
or his ears, or his bald head, or his violet waist-
coat, or his rear embonpoint. Exactly what this
something is, I regret that I cannot tell you. It
remains one of the inexplicable mysteries of un-
applied science, along with the mystery as to why
a man who writes a perfectly legible letter generally signs his name to it in such a hand that no one
can make it out.

§ 16

On Dramatic Chastity.—It is unquestionably
true that Miss Maude Adams' great popular favour was due in no small degree to the fact that
she never appeared in a play in which she was
called upon to be either drunk or criminally as-

saulted. The American public venerates an actress according to her dramatic chastity. Let an actress, however talented, appear in a play, however fine, in which she portrays either a willing or an unwilling victim of sin and soon the public comes to lose its personal affection for her. She may continue to be a box-office card (that is, if her plays are interesting enough), but she cannot keep her position as a public idol. The case of Miss Frances Starr is one in point. Miss Starr had it well within her personal power to become a pet of the playgoing public, but Belasco's protracted casting of her as a kept woman, a girl with a Jekyll-Hyde nature and a seduced convent novice has rendered that power nil. Young Miss Helen Menken will prove another example. She has been violently drunk and deflowered in the small space of four theatrical months. What chance does a poor girl stand after that with a sentimental public?

§ 17

Ziggy.—A year or two back I bade you conjure up the picture of the rotund, rosy, amiable little apple-dumpling, begauded with a facetious derby and an end-man's overcoat, possessed of a brobdingnagian horse-laugh and of the general aspect of Fatty Arbuckle reflected in a trick mirror, who represented then, as he represents still, the finest ideals, the bravest ambitions and the most vigorous analytical and critical virtues to be found in the American dramatic theatre. The portrait was that of Arthur Hopkins. Today, I give you a companion portrait.

If the picture of Hopkins suggests Hi Holler festooned for a pie-eating contest, this companion picture suggests the actor customarily engaged for the rôle of Joe Galvanuzzi, pal of Hop Sing, the villainous Chinaman, in "Followed by Fate." The lavender shirt and collar of the same hue, the purple tie, the socks to match, the sassafras-colour overcoat with belt, the green felt hat, the Italian complexion, the drooping cigarette, the black hair thickly streaked with gray, the general aspect of yon Cassius just after dinner—all are relevantly in it. Passing the subject on the street, one is disappointed not to see him suddenly stop short in his tracks, take three stealthy paces to the left, and hiss. His expression is constantly non-committal; his features are ever as immobile as if he had just been dealt four aces; and his taciturnity as gloomy as if some one else had been dealt a straight flush. He gives one the impression of being habitually seized with a rather wistful stomach-ache; one that, while not painful, is yet sufficiently uncomfortable to make its trustee sad.   I probably have not spoken twenty words to him in my life, and his fifteen or sixteen in reply have been quite as dull and uninteresting as my own.   He prefers Dave Stamper to Beethoven, George V. Hobart to W. S. Gilbert, and Art Hickman to Karl Muck.   And he—"Ziggy" to his help, Florenz Ziegfeld, Jr., to the public—is perhaps the greatest music show producer that the world theatre has thus far known.

This brace of portraits, then, is the pride of the American professional theatre: the one of a man who, more than any other, has brought beauty to its dramatic stage; the other of a man who, more than all the rest combined, has brought beauty to its musical.   Yet the common notion that Ziegfeld is a creator in music show production in the sense that Reinhardt, say, is a creator in dramatic production, is not true.   He is, like Hopkins, an editor.   But, like Hopkins, an editor whose stage editorial skill has lifted the contributions of others to a plane of tripled symmetry, triply smooth rhythm, and tripled loveliness.

Both men stem professionally from the Continent: Hopkins from Germany and the German manner of production, Ziegfeld from France and the French manner.   Study the settings and lightings of Reinhardt and the stage direction of Victor Barnowski, and you find whence the art of Hop-

kins derives.   Study the trick and manner of the
Marigny of 1909 and 1910 and 1911, and you
have a view of the Ziegfeld preparatory school.
But no man ever has improved upon his model
more than this Ziegfeld: his "Follies" and his
"Frolics" are as superior to the Marigny in its
heyday as the Marigny was superior to any other
music hall in Europe.   In every department of
music show production, save one, his stage reaches
its highest level.   In the one department, it reaches
the lowest.   For Ziegfeld's blind spot is the kind
of wit and humorous commentary that have periodically made the French revue famous.   It would
seem that this exceptional professor of the tune
stage knows of no sounder use for two hundred
thousand dollars' worth of magnificent scenes,
costumes, lights and girls than to place them in
their positions upon the stage, crack the whip, and
bid them in combination work themselves up in a
smashing two hour crescendo to a joke about
Henry Ford.   His lighting, his scenery, his costumes and his women are generally exemplary;
his dialogue is usually as witty as a conversation
between two bootleggers.   Even when there comes
to him ready-made something like Rip's immensely
funny satirical burlesque of two youngsters from
the 1920 spring Folies Bergère show, he finds
himself unable to appreciate it, and presents in its

stead a garbled and empty paraphrase wherein for the wit of Rip he substitutes the notion of dressing Miss Ray Dooley in swaddling clothes and then causing her to crack Mr. Charles Winninger over the head with a milk bottle. But aside from this utter banality of dialogue and antic, his stage is a stage on which the light pleasure theatre triumphs as it has never triumphed before.

Until Zeigfeld came upon the scene, the American music show stage (as well as the European) was in the main merely the conventional dramatic stage with a half dozen extra bunchlights set up in the wings and a trap-door cut in the floor large enough to permit De Wolf Hopper to come up through it. It was intrinsically a hybrid stage, a cold stage. Its rhythm was confined to the orchestra pit, its movement to the legs and the diaphragms of the chorus, its charm to the charm of this or that pretty girl. It remained for Ziegfeld to orchestrate it, to take its separate ingredients and fashion them into a warm composition, to put the violins in the girls' legs and the girls' legs in the bull-fiddles, to make the girls melt into the scenes and the scenes melt into the girls. With Ziegfeld, the music show stage became, for the first time in America at least, a clearly individualized stage. Today, it is the stammbühne of its kind the world over.

The Ziegfeld shows are a triumph of overtones. The girls are sometimes inferior to the brand George Edwardes used to display in the London Gaiety; the dancing is sometimes inferior to that in the average Dillingham show; the tunes and lyrics are sometimes inferior to those, say, of the Kern-Wodehouse exhibits; the scenery and lighting are on occasion not better than the scenery and lighting of such a production as Anderson's "What's In a Name?" But the show as a whole is always twice as inveigling and twice as beautiful as any of these. Where the other producers present, Ziegfeld suggests. And in this suggestion, this skimming-over-the water quality, this technique of implication, there is ever a much greater effectiveness than in italics and emphasis. George Edwardes brought out his pretty girls and turned up the lights. Ziegfeld brings out his, and turns down the lights. Dillingham brings out Adele Astaire and lets her dance for fifteen minutes. She dances extremely well. Ziegfeld brings out Mary Eaton and lets her dance one minute. She dances only fairly well. But a minute of moderately good dancing always leaves a better uncritical impression than fifteen minutes of very good dancing. Anderson brings out an elaborately handsome Japanese screen scene and lets the audience look at it for almost half an hour. Ziegfeld brings out a comparatively simple embroidered curtain that no sooner tickles the eye than it is drawn aside to make place for another.

The Ziegfeld technique is the caviare technique, as opposed to the planked steak technique of his competitors. The latter set out to gorge their audiences, to give them a meal; the former gives them just enough to make them thirsty. The "Ziegfeld Follies" arouses curiosity; the "Greenwich Village Follies" satisfies it. From the moment one puts foot in the lobby of the theatre where a Ziegfeld show is playing and lays an eye upon the frieze of chorus girls photographically virginized by Alfred Cheney Johnston, the Ziegfeld hocus-pocus is observable. From the moment one again puts foot in the lobby on the way out to the accompaniment of a boozy, half-asleep melody, the hocus-pocus is memorialized. Ziegfeld, in a word, has adapted the Belasco abracadabra and electrobiology to the more relevant and appropriate field of the music show stage. He has borrowed Little Bright Eyes from the spiritual world, dressed her in thin black silk stockings and pink garters, and put her on the job in the physical.

But—what's it all about, after all?, ask the professors. For all the undoubted proficiency of the fellow, what's the end; what's the use; what's the good? The answer is peculiarly simple. If drama is art in so far as it teaches us to understand life, such a music show is art in so far as it teaches us to enjoy life. I, for one, have never been able to reconcile myself to the notion that a shot like this which gratifies primarily the æsthetic sense, and gratifies it soundly, isn't to be taken as seriously as a drama which gratifies primarily the intellectual. You, perhaps, may get out of Maeterlinck's "The Bethrothal," Augustus Thomas' "As a Man Thinks" or Percy Mackaye's "George Washington" a greater aesthetic, emotional and intellectual lift than you get out of "The Follies," but I don't. If, on the other hand, I get something out of a drama like "Lonely Lives" that I don't get out of a "Follies," I also get something out of the latter that I don't get out of the former. The theory that there may not be as much cultivated beauty in a music show as in a drama has always seemed to me much like a theory that would maintain that the objective beauty of Michelaneglo is inevitably and necessarily less beautiful than, and inferior to, the subjective and spiritual beauty of Dante.

The art of gaiety is an art no less than the art of gloom. Cabell and Ziegfeld are in their separate ways no less artists than Dostoievski and Stanislavski. Anything that can make the Yankee concern himself with beauty is salubrious, even if the beauty is less that of Chopin, Velasquez and Pater than that of Chopin paraphrased, Urban and trim ankles. Even Chopin jazzed is better than Hubbell straight. The persuasion of the American even to beautiful colours, beautiful costumes, beautiful women and beautiful legs is something. It is the first step. It is the sprinkling-can upon a dry and dusty soul. The greenhorn who has been taught to admire a smash of colour, a swish of silks and satins, a lovely face and a smooth ankle is ready for better, and higher, things. The fibrils of beauty are beginning to sprout in him. And slowly, painfully, over the rocky road whereon his successive cultural mileposts are Urban, Rosa Bonheur, Landseer and Millet, and the Swiss bell ringers, John Philip Sousa, Tosti and Massenet, he will mayhap finally and in perspiring triumph arrive at the Mona Lisa and the William Tell overture. If Ziegfeld does not inculcate the love of beauty in the yokel, he at least inculcates the seed of that love. Even a stock-broker, leaving a Ziegfeld show, cannot remain wholly insensible to its callæsthetic pull. Let him have six or eight years of Ziegfeld training and he will perhaps even arrive at the point where he is enthusiastic over Leonard Merrick.

Several years ago, the late Paul Potter was visiting with Thomas Hardy. The latter had not been in a theatre for thirty years. "Let us go to-night," suggested Potter. "What shall we see?" "A musical show," replied Hardy. After the show—it was a revue at the Alhambra largely modelled after and cabbaged from Ziegfeld—Hardy was all excitement. "Fine, fine!" he exclaimed. "Fine and beautiful!" Contrast with this view of the sensitive artist the view of the amiable dolts who see in a show of this kind not life and colour, perfect design and fluid grace, but only Dolores' thighs and Gilda Gray's umbilicus. It would seem that the female figure that indirectly made a peculiar public regard Bouguereau as an artist has rather cryptically made the same peculiar public directly regard Ziegfeld only as a fog-horn.

I have mentioned George Edwardes. It was the trick of this Edwardes to make the girl show lady-like. It is the trick of Ziegfeld to make it glamorous. Before the inauguration of Edwardes, the average music show girl, for all her prettiness, had a sophisticated, hard-enamelled look. Edwardes dressed and conjured the girl so that she looked as if butter wouldn't melt in her mouth. He removed passion from the music show stage, and sagaciously substituted for it the thrice-sensuous innocence. Ziegfeld, as I have once before pointed out, steers the doubly shrewd middle course in bringing sophistication and innocence into sudden, violent and hence effective collision.

To appreciate Ziegfeld, all that one has to do is to view the efforts of his American and European imitators. Even when the latter buy from him his scenes, his costume plates, his tunes, his dance numbers and some of his girls, even when they come over here and personally study his method of composition, even when they contract with his producing help to sail over the sea and assist them closely to duplicate his shows, even then they always find that something very important is lacking. Which very important something is the M. Ziggy.

§ 18

The Love Scene.—The more I think it over, the more I come to believe that the episode between the two young people in the second act (I believe it is the second) of Harvey O'Higgins' and Harriet Ford's failure of several years ago, "Mr. Lazarus," constitutes the most freshly and accurately observed and the most deftly executed love scene in the whole catalogue of American drama. This scene, you may recall, is pitched in the vein of easy comedy: it is love in terms of laughter rather than in the stereotyped terms of soft words, ninny gulps and snifflings. It is fashioned of charming

—and very real—materials. I do not know its
equal in the native theatre.

§ 19

La Dernière Comédie de Don Rostand.—I
allude, obviously enough, to "La Dernière Nuit de
Don Juan," a play profoundly born, profoundly
wise, and profoundly beautiful. Three times in
nine months I have read it, and three times, intoxicated by its beauty, I have found myself periodically raising my eyes from the manuscript and
pausing to address to myself a glowing critical
soliloquy. For here are the laughter and tears
of genius woven into a great, gay ache— a super-
Schnitzlerian tapestry shot through with the brilliant threads of fancy, poetry and sardonic pathos.
For here are literature and drama inextricably
intertwined: a masterpiece of the modern theatre.
Like fine drama of its kind ever, there is something remote about the play. You make to touch
it with your fingers, and it is not there. It is a
mood on the wind, springtime melting into summer
and fading into autumn in the span of a moment.
From the time its Don Juan re-climbs the steps
of Hell to enjoy his respite in the world of women
—repeating with each upward step the name of
Ninon . . . Laura . . . Armande . . . Jeanne

—to the time the devil metes out to him his ironic punishment as the reincarnation of Punchinello in a traveling marionette show—from beginning to end it is as present, and yet as elusive, as the memory of a forgotten tune. Its episodes are a succession of dramatic jewels.

Where Molière's "Le Festin de Pierre" ends, Rostand's work begins. (The prologue has been reconstructed from the author's notes, and is only an outline.) The play carries its central character through scene after scene of wit, charm and tender derisory philosophy. Beside it, all the Don Juan plays ever written, from Zamora's to Grabbe's, and from Molière's to Tellez's and those of the modern continental comedy school of Hans Otto, von Schmitz and Thaddeus Rittner, take on a varying sense of imaginative pallor. Rostand's is an infinitely impudent, infinitely dreamful, infinitely delicate Don Juan. "I am of another essence than your Doctor Faust who wished nothing better than a little German girl," he boasts;—"A town of love has watched my natal day; my dying day should see a town of love. Only one epitaph is fitting for Don Juan: 'He was born at Seville and died at Venice!'" he dreams;—"I have traveled everywhere, like a fairy tale," and his words are fragile and far away . . . Rostand's Don Juan is at once a wit, a philosopher and a child. "One is burned when one has said 'I love you,' " he reminds Punch. "Then how is it done?" asks Punch. "By nudging her? By making eyes?" "That is too stupid; 'tis too carp-like," replies Don Juan. "How should I look?" then Punch. "Like a chasm," replies Don Juan.

Here is Rostand's indomitable Aiglon, grown mature, and off the field of Mars and in the court of Venus: "I am a monster with a soul, a wild-beast archangel, who has preserved, in his fall, his wing." Here is Rostand's Chantecler in doublet and hose: "I am the nostalgia of all. There is no work—despite your hissing, oh ancient adder— no virtue, no science and no faith which does not regret it is not I." "What," asks the devil, "will remain of that?" And Rostand's Cyrano with the small nose answers, "That which remains of Alexander's ashes, and knows that it was Alexander!"

For sheer poetic loveliness there are a half dozen scenes in the play that are not surpassed in modern dramatic literature. Of these all, most noteworthy perhaps is the scene wherein the devil tears into as many small pieces the list of Don Juan's one thousand and three conquests and sends them, like snow, out upon the moonlit bosom of the Adriatic, there each suddenly to be transformed into a gondola bearing the spirit of the woman

whose name was written thereon. I say most
noteworthy, and promptly doubt my words. For
even finer is the ensuing scene wherein the thousand
shadows of silver blue mount silently the stair-
way to challenge and torment Don Juan's memory
of them—he cannot penetrate their masks, their
masks of what passed for love, and blindly, des-
perately, he searches face upon face—it is . . .
it is . . . it is—to the curtain fall. And finer,
more beautifully imagined still, are the scenes
wherein the shadows slowly, derisively, yet tenderly, strip Don Juan of his amorous gasconade
and wherein Don Juan, at the devil's bidding,
collects in a frail chalice the frozen tear-drop
that each shadow wears, like a jewel, in the corner
of her mask—which tears the devil, peering through
an enormous lens, then ironically analyses.

The life of the theatre lies in plays like this.
For one such, a thousand deadly evenings are
gladly endurable. Such episodes as that of the
secret tear, the only one the devil may not touch,
the tear of pity for Don Juan; such profound
mockery as the paint and canvas hell to which
the still strutting Don Juan is in the end consigned;
such humour as lies in Don Juan's pathetic serenity
before the cavalcade of his shadow loves, and
such poetry as lies in the one white fragment of

the torn list—these are the stuff of a glorified and imperishable theatre.

§ 20

George M. Cohan.—George M. Cohan's talent as a playwright is founded not upon an observation and understanding of human nature, but upon an observation and understanding of theatrical nature. He is concerned not with man as man, but with man as member of a theatre audience. How man thinks, acts, dreams, loves and hates in the world does not interest him one-tenth so much as how man reacts to an actor thinking, acting, dreaming, loving and hating on the stage. Human nature, Mr. Cohan shrewdly realizes, ceases to be human nature to a considerable extent soon after handing its ticket to the doorman. The man sitting in an orchestra chair is a somewhat different creature from the man who got out of the taxicab in front of the theatre a few minutes before. He has become, volitionally of course, artificialized to a degree. He has placed himself in what is called the "theatre mood," which is as different from his actual, worldly mood as red is different from green. To attempt, therefore, to treat this man as a rational work-a-day human being is senseless. This, Mr. Cohan appreciates as do few

popular American playwrights. Most of these
playwrights corrupt their popular plays with attempts at the kind of observation, deduction and
philosophy that are part and parcel of a much
more exalted form of drama. And the result is
plays that are neither successfully popular nor of
sound artistic merit. They fall between two
stools.

Mr. Cohan, on the contrary, writes his popular
plays with but one thing in mind, to wit, that they
shall appeal to the artificialized man in the popular-play frame of mind. This does not, as Mr.
Cohan's Broadway contemporaries at times appear
to believe, necessarily mean a man who is incapable of appreciating a higher form of drama. It
may mean simply a man who likes a bit of agree-
ably light and unimportant entertainment now and
then by way of change. The man who sees "Hamlet" on Monday evening and "The Sunken Bell"
on Tuesday evening, and who enjoys both immensely, may enjoy "Seven Keys to Baldpate" on
Wednesday evening even more than the kind of
man who, on the two previous evenings, has gone
to a burlesque show and a play by Mr. Jules
Eckert Goodman. Unlike so many of his Broadway colleagues, Mr. Cohan has the sagacity neither
to write down to the man in the popular-play frame
of mind nor to write over what is—when that man

has placed himself in this frame of mind—his head. The average man who goes to a popular play wants a popular play, just as the average man who goes to a brewery goes there for a glass of beer. The man, whoever or whatever he is, who goes to "Turn to the Right" or "The Bat" wants that kind of play; he doesn't want either a play that tries to be popular and can't—like "Desert Sands," say, on the one hand—or a play that tries to be unpopular and succeeds—like "Difference in Gods," say, on the other.

Mr. Cohan gives such a man exactly what he wants, or at least makes it his business to try to give him exactly what he wants. He does not, like his colleagues, show off with attempts at sharp character drawing, with moral purpose, with sense, with flights of fancy, with philosophies of life or with any other such pieces of excess baggage. He has studied the human being in the audience long enough to know that that human being, once he is in the theatre, is less a human being than an actor, so to speak, in street clothes: a harmless and somewhat idiotic creature with his eye winking and his mind in his necktie, interested not nearly so much in dramatic accuracy and vraisemblance as in pleasant nonsense. Nine men in ten look on the theatre as a "party"; the tenth goes to the Neighbourhood Play-

house. Mr. Cohan is essentially a "party" playwright. He gets, figuratively, a bit tipsy, trips up
the butler, pours the bowl of goldfish into the
piano, slaps the hostess on the back, whistles the
Greek national anthem, takes a running slide across
the ballroom floor, knocks over half a dozen palms,
and lands on the bass drum with the drummer on
top of him. Which is a picture of the average
George Cohan play.

§ 21

Paradox.—Why it is that in the middle of summer a music show theatre always seems cooler
than a dramatic theatre, I don't know. Surely
there is no sound reason for the phenomenon.
Surely the spectacle of a music show cast of one
hundred men and women galloping about the
stage half dead with perspiration should not be
so cooling as the spectacle of a dramatic cast of
six or seven persons lolling calmly in chairs and
upon couches. It is one of the insoluble riddles,
along with why a man with his linen collar off
always looks warmer than a man with his linen
collar on, even though both may be equally cool.
It cannot be that the hotter the object one looks
at the cooler one feels one's self. If this were
true, the sight of a blazing grate would cause one
to shiver.

§ 22

Emperor William in Exile.—Every once in so
often it becomes necessary for a dramatic critic
to write about Shakespeare if for no other reason
than to meet his readers' notion of what constitutes
his dignity and scholarly footing. The duller he
writes, the more dignified and scholarly he is considered. More critics have gained good repu-
tations with bad essays on Shakespeare than one
can remember. No Englishman accepted Shaw
seriously as a critic until Frank Harris took Shaw's
articles on Shakespeare and showed how bad they
were. Of all subjects concerned with drama and
the theatre Shakespeare is the only one about which
one may write idiotically with security. It is
just as safe, and just as profound, to argue that
Hamlet was crazy as to argue that he wasn't. They
may contradict you, but they can't prove absolutely
that you are wrong. If anyone contended that
Paula Tanqueray's moodiness was due to a serious
case of persistent glucosuria, he would promptly
be set down either as a poor comedian or an imbecile. But let the same person contend that Iago's
machinations were undoubtedly prompted by sex
suppression and he is forthwith hailed as the pro-
pounder of a New Theory.

Let us not too soon deplore the levity of such

an approach to the subject. There is more sound criticism in Huneker's "Old Fogy" than in the complete works of Henry T. Finck, including the footnotes. The Archduke trio is a grander thing on three cocktails and a pony of Chartreuse than on a plate of sirloin. The best criticism of the contemporary French drama is to be found in the farces of Sacha Guitry; and I am not at all certain, for all the estimable Archer's view to the contrary, that there isn't a much sharper criticism of American life in the farce comedies of the George M. Cohan school than in nine-tenths of the more sober plays written during their time. The deathlessness of Shakespeare is a tribute to the deadliness of the thousands of essays written on him. The mortality of a minor poet—say Maeterlinck—is predicated on the complete ease with which lively and interesting essays may be written on him. Genius is the capacity for making others take infinite pains.

I have read perhaps nearly all that has been written of Shakespeare in English, French and German, and, with six notable exceptions, there isn't among all this puffing, pulling and straining one-half the measure of truly revelatory criticism that one finds in the facile, offhand little articles on Maeterlinck by Clarence Day, Jr., and André Tridon. Jules Lemaître has said that a work of

genius has for its authors the poet himself in the
first place and later the most original of his readers
in the course of generations. "This," he observed, "is truer of Shakespeare than of any other
writer. His works might be entitled, 'Complete
Works of Shakespeare, by William Shakespeare
and by all the poets and critics, French, German
and English, for eighty years.'" One might wish
that Lemaître had written "in spite of" in place of
the second "by." For one Harris, Shakespeare
has had a thousand Paul Bourgets.

According to the advertisements that appeared
at the time in the newspapers, Mr. Arthur Hopkins
not so very long ago produced Shakespeare's "Macbeth." A view of the exhibit convinced one, however, that it was not Mr. Arthur Hopkins who produced Shakespeare's "Macbeth" so much as it was
Shakespeare's "Macbeth" that produced Mr. Arthur Hopkins. It was difficult to discern any
Shakespeare, save in the audience. The stage disclosed a minimum of Shakespeare and a maximum
of Hopkins. In an announcement made preliminary to the production, Mr. Hopkins affirmed that
it was his intention to present the play for its enduring values alone. "My intention," he stated in
effect, "will be to release the immortal theme from
the text, without regard for time or place or people." In a manner of speaking, Mr. Hopkins may

be said to have succeeded brilliantly. He not only
released from the text the immortal theme, but almost everything else that Shakespeare put into it.
I lay the blame on poor Mr. Hopkins, though the
truth is that if ever a scene designer, composer of
incidental music and leading actor betrayed a
producer, the Messrs. Robert Edmond Jones, Robert
R. Bennett and Lionel Barrymore did that very
thing. Jones' scenery fought the Hopkins direction
at every turn; Bennett impudently essayed to make
the music of Shakespeare more musical by adding
to it a couple of cornets and a bass viol; and Barrymore's Macbeth was merely the villain in an old
Theodore Kremer melodrama, minus only the
patent leather shoes, silk hat and black moustache.
Hopkins' guilt as a theatrical producer rests chiefly
in his having taken "Macbeth" out of the theatre
and put it back into the library. It is one of this
producer's virtues that he can take a modern play
that is in some measure purely "theatre" and, by
extracting from it that share of theatricality, give
it the smooth feel of life. But when he visits this
same technique upon a play like "Macbeth," one
that is entirely "theatre," he ruins the play by introducing contact with life into it. It cannot profit
an artificial flower, however beautiful, to plant it
in the soil of earth. "Macbeth" is simply an old
A. H. Woods thriller written by the greatest poet

that ever lived. It should be played just as an old A. H. Woods thriller would be played, by the greatest actors that ever lived. To play it as if it were "A Successful Calamity" is to play "Shenandoah" like "The Yellow Jacket."

Mr. Jones, for all the unanimous admission that he went far astray in the present instance, has been credited in many quarters with having nevertheless exercised great imagination in his settings for the production, and has been complimented for his habitual "initiative" and "artistic courage." Though it is true that this Mr. Jones has done more for the beauty of American theatrical investiture than any other man, and though it is equally true that his work in "Richard III" marked the high level for this country, his much spoken of imagination in the case of "Macbeth" was actually less imagination than lack of imagination. In American criticism almost everything is called imaginative that substitutes mere novelty or freakishness for authentic fancy. There is, of course, a very high degree of imagination that finds itself allied with integrity to novelty and freakishness—as in the case of, say, Strindberg and his "Dream Play"—but Mr. Jones' imagination in the instance of "Macbeth" was imagination primarily in terms of hallucination. The reason is perhaps not far to seek. Mr. Jones is a highly talented man in his own right, but he is gradually being goaded beyond his capabilities by his overzealous admirers. One of these admirers has written of his work in the production under consideration, "Certainly nothing approaching it in radical originality has been seen on any established stage in this country or Europe." If this sort of thing keeps up, poor Mr. Jones will be Ben-Ami'd before he is much older. He is a skilful designer—the best we have —but his is fundamentally not an original mind, and it is a pity to urge him to an originality that is not in him and that, in the mad groping for it, brings him to abandon the very considerable talent for imitative beauty that he possesses. His work in "Macbeth," so far as "radical originality" goes, was radically original only in so far as it combined the radicality of such familiar German scenic artists as Ludwig Sievert and W. Wirk with the originality of Gordon Craig, a combination of theories akin to a commixture of Gertrude Stein and Shelley. That this commingling of theories was deliberate on Mr. Jones' part is hardly to be doubted, since his studies in Germany surely made him privy to the devices of both Sievert and Wirk, and since his fundamental theory of investiture is, and always has been, of a piece with Craig's. Had he directly imitated either Sievert or Wirk on the

one hand or Craig, their father, on the other, his
"Macbeth" would have been a valuable effort.
The strain for originality was what deleted the
effort of all of its value. Mr. Hopkins had best
bear Jones closely in mind in the matter of future
productions. Beginning as of one mind, they are
gradually pulling apart from each other in theory.
Jones will ruin Hopkins and Hopkins Jones, unless they soon get together and make common
ground.

Mr. Hopkins, like many producers who have
attempted to bring new interpretations to Shakespeare, similarly broke himself on the rocks of
originality. In his effort to steer a middle course
between the Craig theory on the one side and the
Expressionism theory on the other, he ran on the
shoals of a nondescript island peopled entirely by
Robert Mantells and Walter Hasenclevers. In his
commendable attempt to break away from the
American papier-mâché Shakespearian tradition—
the Shakespeare of pulpit elocution, Bryan gestures, canvas castles and Columbia sophomore
Romans—he broke away not only from the American Shakespeare but from the Stratford Shakespeare as well. For there is a deal of Shakespeare
that demands just this banal treatment for its best
theatrical effect. I am surely not ass enough to
argue that there is only one way to play Shakes-

peare, but I can never quite rid myself of the conviction that a combination of what is best in the
traditional way and of what is best in the new is
not the most satisfactory way.   This was the plan
of Reinhardt, to whom the theatre owes several of
its finest Shakespearean productions.   This is the
way of Gordon Craig, for all his wish to deny it.
Craig has simply rid tradition of its ugliness, preserved what was beautiful in it, and given that
beauty a twofold life with the blood of a vivid
and pulsing fancy.   Strindberg's "Shakespeare is
as formless as a rigid and pedantic formalist" may
be made to apply to the productions of Shakespeare as well as to the plays themselves.   There
was more of the traditional Shakespeare in Mr.
Hopkins' production of "Richard III," an admirable production if ever there was one, than Mr.
Hopkins himself perhaps suspects.

§ 23

*The Dramatic Imagination of Augustus
Thomas.*—The dramatic imagination of Augustus
Thomas, roughly speaking, falls into two clas-
sifications.   The first classification is that which has
produced works like "Arizona" and "Rio Grande"
in which Mr. Thomas has sought to conceal the
banality of the old French triangle play by dress-

ing up the characters in United States military uni-
forms and naming the back-drop after an American
state or precinct. The second is that which has
produced works like "As a Man Thinks" and "The
Model" in which Mr. Thomas has sought to conceal
the banality of the old French triangle play by
giving it an overtone of Christian Science, psy-
choanalysis, hypnotism, idiopathic epilepsy and
veterinary surgery, to say nothing of atavism,
thought transference, osteopathy and the mor-
phology of the sound-transmitting apparatus in
caudate amphibia and its phylogenetic significance.
His most recent work, "Nemesis," comes in the
main under the latter classification, for here again
is the old Gymnase prosaic husband-young wife-
romantic artist triangle tricked out with a false
bottom and put over on the audience with much
monkey business anent psychiatry, the fallibility
of finger-print evidence, empirical psychology,
psycho-neurology and psychozoic phenomena
generally, to say nothing of Mr. Thomas' customary further demonstration of cultured ignorance
which imposes upon him a sophomoric delight in
soberly unloading upon his hearers the results
of his somewhat tardy delvings into Epaminondas,
Virgil, Dante, De Quincey, Freud and Bernard
Shaw.

It is now some sixteen years that Mr. Thomas

stopped writing plays and began writing college
entrance examinations in dramatic form. His
stage exhibits since that time have, with one or
two exceptions, seemed like nothing so much as
explosions in small town second-hand book stores,
littering the neighbourhood with yellowed frag-
ments of the encyclopedias and scientific text
books of thirty years ago. It has apparently become impossible for Mr. Thomas to write a simple
love scene without learnedly including in it at least
one allusion to Gaspar de la Cerda Sandoval Silva
y Mendoza, the Pterideæ, or the differential features between melanosis and melanosarcoma. If
one of his characters pulls out a revolver, the other
promptly comes back at him with a snappy reference to Diphenyltetrachlorophthalide or "Tristan and Isolde." If a husband surprises his wife
in flagrante delicto with her lover, does he land a
reverberating boot upon the latter's seat, or run
him through the colon, or ruin his nose? He does
not. He demolishes the fellow by delivering a
twenty-minute address on gastroenterostomy, Zoo-
logische Forschungsreisen in Australien, Camille
Flammarion, the relative advantages of the use of
sodium and potassium hydroxides in the prepara-
tion of alkaline pyrogallol, and the financial condition of the Gouverneur and Oswegatchie Railroad Company . . .

§ 24

The Lesser British Playwrights.—One of the weaknesses of the lesser British playwrights of the day lies in the omnipresent dodge of attempting to brew laughter from the ancient device of bringing into sharp juxtaposition two subjects violently out of key with each other. An irrelative allusion to pigs interjected suddenly into a conversation on love, an alien reference to sausages inserted into an observation on cynicism, an extraneous mention of a bowler hat during a discussion of poetry —these are the species of comic gold-fish that such playwrights as A. A. Milne, for example, continually pull out of their silk hats. And when they do not rely upon sudden contrast as a comic device, their reliance is largely upon such equally fragile devices as causing a comic character to repeat the remark of a serious character directly after him, mispronouncing a person's name, and confusing Eugene Aram with Enoch Arden. These playwrights suffer further from their heavy effort to be insistently light. Their lightness has about it not infrequently a sense of tug and strain. Where British playwrights like the late Haddon Chambers or Hubert Henry Davies, appreciating their shortcomings, promptly abandoned froth qua froth the moment they detected a bead of perspiration upon

its brow, the lesser writers of today blandly wipe
off the bead and plough determinedly ahead.
The net impression that one takes away from their
exhibits is, consequently, of having been present
at a dinner party whereat all the exceptionally
dull guests have endeavoured to be assiduously
amusing.

§ 25

The French and American Points of View—
Whenever a new risqué farce is produced we are
sure to be entertained with more or less indignant
blabber on the difference between the French and
American points of view. It is the custom on
these occasions to contend that where a certain
species of episode may be quite all right for the
French, it is not quite all right for the American,
since the American does not look on sex as the
Frenchman does. Granting that this is true,
which it isn't, what argument could yet be more
stupid? The circumstance that the French as a nation regard sex much more lightly than the Americans as a nation surely can have nothing to do
with the American's theatrical taste for sex lightly
regarded. As well argue the other way round
and say that because the American regards sex
much more seriously than the French, the French-

man cannot theatrically abide sex thus presented.
The question is wholly removed from the theatre.
An American audience just as often turns a sex
farce like "Fair and Warmer" into a great success as a French audience turns a serious play
like "Le Voleur." And to imagine that were outright adultery to be incorporated into a sex farce
like "Fair and Warmer" the American audience
(unlike the French) would have nothing to do with
the farce is to ask us to imagine that an audience
that crowds an American theatre in search of
naughtiness would be insulted and outraged if
it got what it went to find. Any adultery farce
that was well enough written would succeed in
America. Adultery farces fail in France just as
often as farces with the adultery expurgated fail
in America, and for the same reason. It is a
question, in both cases, not of adultery or expurgated adultery, but of the vigour of the farce itself.

The notion, further, that the French regard sex
chiefly as a kind of Coney Island is anything but
true. A certain class of Parisian regards it thus,
just as does a certain class of New Yorker. But
the average Frenchman is not much different from
the average resident of Hoboken. There is, accordingly, no contemporary theatre that houses
so many dramas dealing with sex as a profound

business as the French theatre. Look over the
list of plays presented in the French theatres during the last twelve or fifteen years and consider
the enormous number of serious sex dramas produced by de Curel, Hervieu, Donnay, Brieux,
Armory, Lavedan, Bernstein, Bataille, Bisson, de
Croisset, Mirbeau, Trarieux, Rochard, de Nion,
Porto-Riche, Decourcelle, Delard, the Marguer-
itte brothers, Wolff, Tristan Bernard (in such plays
as "Sa Soeur"), Bourget, Aderer, Ephraim, Roths-
child, and half a hundred others. Try to find an
equal number in the theatre of any other country!
Try, for instance, to find half the number in the
American theatre that is supposed by the logi-
cians to be especially hospitable to this serious
sex point of view.

Times change, and we change with them. A
dirty sex farce like "The Girl With the Whooping
Cough" packs a Garrick Theatre in Philadelphia
to the doors, where a clean serious sex drama like
"The Shadow" (even with the popular Ethel
Barrymore) starves to death in a theatre down the
street. "Up in Mabel's Room" plays to capacity
at the Park Square in Boston after a series of advance newspaper advertisements showing a girl in
bed with the caption "Such a Funny Feeling,"
while a Pinero serious sex drama plays to empty
rows in the next block. "Twin Beds," "His

Bridal Night," "The Girl in the Limousine" and "The Demi-Virgin" crowd the Broadway theatres while sex soberly treated by Tolstoi, Hauptmann and others timidly plays up some side-street or alley to a handful of semi-aliens. The American audience, in short, cherishes a dirty farce every bit as much as the French audience—more, I should say. Mr. A. H. Woods has made twenty times as much money out of loud sex farce as any three Parisian producers combined. And I do not overlook, in the latter category, such uniformly successful Parisian light sex caterers as the younger Guitry.

§ 26

The Smile Versus The Laugh.—Charles Frohman insisted throughout his producing career that there was no money in what he called "a smile play," that is, a play that provoked merely smiles and not laughter. Charles Frohman for thirty years produced his plays upon this principle. And Charles Frohman died a poor man. . . . Laugh and the world laughs with you; smile and you smile alone. This, the doctrine that lost Charles Frohman so much of his money. And the irony of it is that the doctrine is true.

An American theatrical audience does not want to smile; it wants to undo its top trouser button and let go.   It will spend three hundred thousand dollars to laugh at "Fair and Warmer," but it will not spend a cent to smile at "The Steamship Tenacity." Frohman went nigh bankrupt because, though his credo was sound, his talent for differentiating between the smile and the laugh was not. He often produced serious plays so comically and comic plays so seriously that he confused his customers. They found themselves smiling when they should have laughed, and laughing when they should have smiled.   After a few years of this sort of thing they became so embarrassed that they gave up Frohman, and moved bag and baggage across the street to A. H. Woods.   But although there is more theatrical money to be made out of laughter than out of smiles, this does not prove that laughter is superior to the smile any more than the fact that there is more money to be made out of "Don't Kiss Me on the Nose, Dearie; My Dog Has Spanish Blood" than out of "Sardanapale" proves that Berlin is superior to Berlioz.   The smile is the true aristocrat of dramatic literature; the laugh is the peasant.   The smile is a child of the intelligence; the laugh is a child of the belly. "Gentlemen smile; their valets laugh," wrote Lord Chesterfield.   Christ smiled, but did not laugh. We know from the records that Caesar and Napoleon smiled, but there is no record of their

laughter.   George Washington, it appears, smiled;
Warren Gamaliel Harding, we know, laughs. . . .

What America needs is more smilers and less
laughers.   There is too much laughter in the country.   Go into a railway smoking car and a dozen
Elks are hard at it.   Go into a restaurant and two
dozen drummers and manicure girls are neighing
like jackasses.   Go to Washington and you find
the entire coloured population laughing itself half
to death over the Administration.   Go into a theatre
and a houseful of emotional Dadaists is bellowing
at the spectacle of a fat comedian trying to hide
himself in a phonograph box.   There is a gar-
gantuan laughter for "The Cruise of the Kawa,"
but there are too few smiles for "Jurgen."   There
is a roar for Frank Tinney, but there are not enough
smiles for Maurice Baring.   The cocktail may
have followed the flag once upon a time, but taste
in America has never followed laughter.   Taste
and perception follow the smile.   One laughs at
Topsy, "Charley's Aunt" and Woodrow Wilson,
much as one laughs at a man who sits upon a
tack; but one smiles at Tartufe, "The Last Night
of Don Juan" and Arthur Balfour, much as one
ever smiles at something wistful in its superiority.
They smile in Downing Street; they laugh at
Bloomingdale.

The American laughter at "The Demi-Virgin"

has a million times the voltage of the American smiles at "Anatol." The laughter over "Billy Baxter's Letters" has a million times the voltage of the smiles over "The Revolt of the Angels." Taste coughs its way to a phthisical death, and the mourners have to bite their tongues to still their loud chuckles. Consider the theatre. What is the quality of the plays that provoke the loudest and most commercially profitable laughter? I give a few more recent examples: "Getting Gertie's Garter," "Six-Cylinder Love," "Bluebeard's Eighth Wife," "Thank You," "Captain Applejack," "Lilies of the Field," and "Kiki." Again, what is the quality of the plays that provoke but smiles, alas unprofitably? I give a few more recent examples: Gribble's "March Hares," Bataille's "Don Juan," Lennox Robinson's "The White-Headed Boy," de Caillavet's and de Flers' "The Fan," Brieux's "Madame Pierre," Courteline's "Boubouroche," the aforementioned Vildrac's "S. S. Tenacity." . . .

The easiest thing in the world is to make a theatre-goer laugh. He will laugh when a black-face comedian turns around for the thousandth time and discloses two large white pearl buttons sewed upon the seat of his pants. He will laugh when the same comedian trips over an imaginary object and, regaining his balance, purses his mouth

in an effeminate manner and says "Oh sassafras!"
He will laugh when anyone alludes to a Ford automobile or Carter's Little Liver Pills, to an onion,
a prune or a Congressman, to wood alcohol or
William Jennings Bryan, to the holes in dough-
nuts, socks and Swiss cheese, to hell or Yonkers,
to Gatti-Casazza, frankfurter sausages, spaghetti,
Trotski, apple sauce, cabbage (if only it be pro-
nounced cab-bah-ge), the Erie railroad, the New
York, New Haven and Hartford or the B. and O.,
to Altoona, Pa., or a dill pickle, to September
Morn or the Albany Night Boat, to anyone named
Oswald, Rudolph, Clarence or Percy, to Philadelphia, the police force or Limburger cheese, to the
telephone service, Meyerbeer, the *Ladies' Home
Journal*, lobsters, ear muffs, insufficient bathing,
the "Götterdämmerung," rhubarb, alfalfa, Pittsburgh, or to several thousands of other such phenomena. But the matter of making him smile is
reserved for artists—that is, if a smile is not beyond his learning. Yet beyond his talent such
smiles apparently are—and what he misses! The
rare smiles of Bahr's "Master," of Molnar's
"Phantom Rival," of Galsworthy's "Pigeon," of
Barrie's "Legend of Leonora," of a score of
delightful things—all rapidly sent into the theatrical discard by our herd of humourless laughers,

§ 27

The Yiddish Drama.—The enthusiastic criticisms of Peretz Hirshbein's "The Idle Inn," composed by the local reviewers when the play was produced in its original tongue in the Jewish Art Theatre, were plainly due to the deception that a foreign tongue in drama always works upon uncomprehending ears. A play always seems better than it actually is in a language that one doesn't understand. I am certain, for example, that my own original enthusiasm for the exhibits in the Moscow Art Theatre was due in considerable measure to the fact that I know only seven words in Russian, five of which haplessly have to do with liquor. There is a peculiar sense of importance to a language with which one is not familiar. If some prankful manager were tomorrow night to produce a play by Samuel Shipman down on the Bowery in Polish, it is morally certain that the next morning's newspapers would excitedly hail it as a great masterpiece. "The Idle Inn," allowing for what I am informed by presumably sound judges is a crude translation, is—like much of the Yiddish drama—a hybrid of Russian peasant drama crossed with a Celtic strain. It has a certain agreeable exotic overtone, but its body is imaginatively lethargic and, where not lethargic, often

transparently imitative. It impresses one, with a
few exceptions, merely as bad Dunsany played on
a badly lighted stage.

§ 28

O'Neill and His Critics.—Those critics who are
hostile to Eugene O'Neill contend against him that
he has no saving humour. The same thing may
nine times in ten be said of Hauptmann. I do
not, of course, mean to compare O'Neill with the
great German; but to urge humour upon a dramatist like O'Neill is akin to urging poetry upon one
like George Ade. Again, they contend against
O'Neill that he sees the world too insistently as
the stage of tragedy. If Shakespeare had died
after writing only four of his masterpieces, "Hamlet," "Macbeth," "Romeo" and "Othello," might
not the same thing have been idiotically written of
him? Such criticism of a dramatist seems to me
to be exceedingly silly. If O'Neill had humour it
would probably corrupt his strong, passionate, sardonic and eloquent pessimism, and he would be
writing hybrid pot-boilers like the late Charles
Klein. And if he saw the world as less cloudy
and more golden with sunshine, he doubtless would
be writing "Pegs o' My Heart" instead of "Beyond the Horizons" and "Emperor Joneses" and
"Hairy Apes." But even so, O'Neill's critics

seem to me to view him faultily on these very
points. He has humour. It is not, of course,
the humour that reposes in jokes on bootlegging,
katzenjammer and spinach. It is the ironic humour of an observant and reflective man: the
grim humour that lies at the bottom of man's
eternal tussle with Fate, the conquering clown.
This humour shines brilliantly forth from the
best of O'Neill's work. And again, though his
critics blink it, he has poetry. The general view
of O'Neill's plays as a "realistic" string of sailors'
oaths, deep gutterals, colloquialisms and expector-
ations is anything but accurate. There is dramatic poetry of an unmistakable subtlety in "Beyond the Horizon," in "The Straw" and, above
all, in "The Fountain." In this last named manuscript there is a degree of lovely line as musical
as anything in Stephen Phillips, as clear and
simple and sparkling as a lyric by John McClure.
O'Neill, taking him by and large, stands out from
the run of Americans writing for the stage by virtue of a sullen and aloof independence that steadfastly declines to take into consideration anything
but the manuscript before him. Appropriate actors ready and eager to be remuneratively tailored,
some fetching and promising designs by a scenic
artist, the whole external to-do of the theatre—
none of these things interests him. He remembers

that, save a writer be a great genius, such things are secondary, and so writes his plays with no thought of them. I know of no other American playwright who goes at his work with the consistent and resolute honesty of O'Neill. Sometimes, of course, this consistent and resolute independence produces work that might have been bettered by a bit of clear-visioned and well-reasoned compromise, but more often it produces work that is a fine challenge to the beauty that lies so often buried under the dust of our native stage.

§ 29

In Defense of Plagiarism.—The more often I go to the theatre these nights, the more I am persuaded to believe in plagiarism. In the past I have steadfastly decried it, and have not without absurd heat exposed those of our playwrights who have been guilty of it. But time is a wise teacher, and I have come to change my mind. After sitting through the bulk of original plays that our American playwrights have written lately, I am firmly convinced that it would be much better for our theatre were they to forsake originality and pilfer the work of others.

The originality of the average American playwright is an awe-inspiring thing. It generally

takes some such masterly form as causing the detective, instead of the dissolute nephew, to turn
out to be the murderer, or showing that the pearl
necklace which the crooks have contemptuously rejected as paste is genuine. After a protracted
period of such originality, even the most high-
spirited defender of law and justice is ready to
shout at the top of his lungs for bold and forth-
right plagiarism. This is my present attitude. I
can see no good in holding back longer. Why go
on night after night listening to original American
plays in which Brass-Knuckle Mike is reformed
by Love, in which the persecuted pushcart peddler,
Irving Einstein, is discovered in Act IV to have a
heart of gold and is thereupon promptly elected to
membership in the Union, Brook and Knicker-
bocker clubs, and in which Fleurette Le Clair wins
back her husband Ludwig by outwitting the grass
widow Gonzalez—why, as I say, go on ruining
one's ear-drum with such moonshine when there
are half a hundred toothsome ideas lying around
loose in European plays ready to be cabbaged?
I appreciate, of course, that this is no startlingly
new idea that I advance. A number of our original American playwrights have not only anticipated me, but have already put it into practice.
A few years ago, for instance, I went to see a farce
by one of our original American playwrights that

would have been woefully dull had not the sagacious fellow been wise enough to lift his chief
comic scene from Guitry's "La Prise de Berg-op-
Zoom." By way of another example, I recall having looked at a satirical farce comedy by the same
original playwright—this was a year or two later—
the central idea of which was suspiciously like
that of the German Scholz's satirical farce comedy, "Borrowed Souls." The idea of this latter
play appeared, indeed, to be so appealing that
not only was it cabbaged by one of our geniuses,
but by two. For a third instance, the most amusing comedy of one of our most original play-
makers—a dramatist whose gems illuminate several of the anthologies—is in texture brother to a
comedy that richly entertained the Paris boulevards about eleven years ago.

As a general rule, however, the trouble with
our original playwrights is that, when they have
sufficient modesty to use the ideas of other men,
they make the mistake of seizing upon the poor
ideas of these men and letting the good ones go.
What they need is a schooling in plagiarism, that
they may learn just where the good ideas are.
With my customary sense of constructive criticism, I therefore come to their assistance. An
excellent farce-comedy situation remains to be sto-
len—to give a first example—from the second act

of Rip and Bousquet's "The Habit of a Lackey."
This episode evoked roars of laughter when it
was disclosed to French audiences eight or nine
years ago and, if prudently transferred to an
American setting, would doubtless never be recognized as being other than original by our native
theatrical commentators. By way of reassuring
our playwrights, they need have nothing to fear
in the matter of exposure from these commentators.
As a general rule, the acquaintance that these
gentlemen enjoy with foreign dramatic literature
is limited to the reprints in *L'Illustration*, the re-
sumé of Continental play plots in *Variety*, and the
dramatic department in the Tuesday edition of
The Christian Science Monitor. These do not
cover the field in a way that would be dangerous,
so our playwrights need not suffer profound trepi-
dation. Another good idea may be found in a
German play called "The Forest of Bliss." This
idea, a study in romance as opposed to realism,
would come in very nicely, as would also the idea
of another German play, produced in the Berlin
Kleines-theater in 1913, called "Jettchen Gebert."
Cross the line into France, and still another available idea may be found in the extemely humorous farce of Robert Dieudonné wherein the home
of the hero and his wife and that of the hero and
his mistress are decorated in exactly the same man-

ner, to the befuddlement of the hero in Act II
when he arrives in an elegantly intoxicated condition.   Here in Paris our playwrights may further find an excellent comic situation in the Grand
Guignol play of eight seasons ago entitled "The
Big Match," to say nothing of a second Guignol
sketch named "The Benefactress."   But what do
our original playwrights do?   Instead of bagging
the best ideas of their European confrères, ideas
such as those of Földes, Heltai, Rittner, Gignoux,
Bahr, Paul, et al., they carelessly bag the worst.
Well, not all of them, since we must not forget
that one of them a few years ago lifted Bahr's
"Kinder" almost in toto.   But this, unfortunately,
is a too infrequent occurrence. Usually the American playwright spoils the whole thing by changing
the cabbaged idea a little, and adding to it something original of his own.   Or, when he does not
do this, he shows a weak power of selection, and
picks out an inferior idea in one of the foreign
plays.   He exercises no discrimination whatso-
ever, but takes the first idea that he encounters.
Thus, when he makes an appropriation from Bahr,
he takes "Kinder" and loses sight of "The Yellow
Nightingale."   Thus, when he achieves a steal
from Dreyer, he takes "The Pastor's Daughter of
Streladorf" and overlooks "Three." . . .
The legal or ethical aspects of the matter do

not at the moment concern me. Something must
be done—and done soon—to get the American
drama out of its imaginative doldrums. We must
be patriotic, and get busy. Let no foreign nation
stand in our way! Why was the American theatre
so alive during the late war? Because, under
cover of war and the incidental abrogation of copy-
right laws, our playwrights took unto themselves
whatever they found and liked in Continental theatrical literature. Why should they stop now,
simply because the war has stopped? For any
intelligent answer to which question I offer a
grand prize consisting of a pass to any one of the
following recent strictly original American plays:
"Pot Luck," "The Man in the Making," "Wait
Till We're Married," "Like a King," "Beware of
Dogs," "The Skylark," "The Teaser," "Honours
Are Even," "Sonny," "The Scarlet Man," "The
Triumph of X," "The Detour," "Personality,"
"The Poppy God," "Back Pay," "The Elton Case,"
"Only 38," "The Night Call," "I Will If You
Will," "Fools Errant," "Manhattan," "Lights
Out," "The Charlatan" or "Wild Oats Lane."

§ 30

The Worst Duo.—Superlatives are not always
without their dangers, yet it seems safe to say

that "Uncle Tom's Cabin" is the worst persistently popular novel ever written, and that "Uncle
Tom's Cabin," the play made from that novel,
the worst persistently popular play ever produced.
There is not a thought or line in either that might
not have been imagined and recorded by a delicatessen dealer or a Columbia University professor.

§ 31

The Chauve-Souris and Art.—Nikita Balieff's
Théâtre de la Chauve-Souris, imported from Moscow via Paris via London by Mr. Morris Gest, liai-
son officer of the Russian-American stage, is the
victim of its press-agents. A popular vaudeville
show of varying degree of merit, it has been made
ridiculous through an attempt to exalt it out of all
proportion to its intrinsic qualities. "Its pro-
grams," thus its local sponsors, "have a definite
form and style, and yet a tremendous catholicity;
they indicate research, a profound scholarship (!),
daring and delicate artistry, all brought into perfect harmony. All the resources of aestheticism
are drawn upon—the cultured human voice, pic-
torial art, music, dancing, mimicry—in an endeavour to attain the supreme in art. The Théâtre de la Chauve-Souris is Russian; but it claims
its heritage of literature and art from the uni-

verse." The Keith vaudeville press-agent himself has never been so voluptuous—not even in his advertisements of Doraldina the cooch dancer or Loyal's Trained Dogs.

The "art" nonsense has gone so far in the theatre that nothing is presently more gratifying than the exhibition of something without a falseface, whether it be a nigger music show, a Fourteenth Street burlesque show or—one might even go so far as to say—a play staged by Mr. William A. Brady. Everything is "art" of one kind or another. "The Greenwich Village Follies" has "art" scenery. "Swords" is "artistic" drama "artistically" staged. All the younger producers are eloquently working in the interests of the "art" of the theatre. The only actor who admits that he is not an artist is Ed Wynn. There is not an actress who will admit anything of the sort. All the new theatres are of "artistic" *décor* and design. The stage of the new Earl Carroll playhouse is so full of new art appliances that there is hardly enough space left for the actors to dress in. The composer of "Good Morning, Dearie" writes a letter to the newspapers proving that the score of that august opera is not jazz, but art. The theatrical magazines print long articles on "The Art of Stage Lighting," "The Art of Sam Bernard," "The Art of Costume Designing," "The Art of J.

J. Shubert" and "The Art of Thomas A. Dixon" in
place of the old half-tones of Lotta Faust with a
rose in her mouth, Mazie Follette leaning on a
pedestal, and Bonnie Maginn in strip tights.   The
one manager who says that he is not an artistic
producer is A. H. Woods, and he makes his press-
agent contradict him the next day.   The only thing
that has taken place in the Town Hall in the last
two years that has not been described as art of
one kind or another was the debate on birth control, and that was raided by the police.   Miss
Ruth Draper's monologues are announced as
"sheer art."   Anything in a diaper with a violin
off-stage is "aesthetic dancing."   Mr. Owen Davis
writes "The Detour" and the next morning becomes
an artist-dramatist.   The ushers are dressed like
Watteau shepherdesses or Gainsborough duchesses.
The entr'-acte orchestras play selections from the
art nouveau score of Serge Prokofieff.   Mr.
Archie Selwyn affects the dress of a Latin Quarter
student. . . .

The Chauve-Souris, for all the screen of art
smoke adroitly contrived by its managers, is, as
I have said, nothing more than a simon-pure vaudeville show with a Russian flavour.   I use the word
vaudeville in its American meaning and with its
American implications.   Consider a few items on
its initial bill.   No. I is called "Porcelaine de

Saxe" and is the familiar tableau of the two porce-
lain figures that presently come to life, embrace,
pirouette, and stiffen again upon the striking of
the clock—a favourite bit in the Lilliputians' "Magic Doll," produced in the early '90's. No. II is
"Songs by Glinka."   No. III is "The Parade of
the Wooden Soldiers," Fred Walton's old act and,
unless my memory is bad, once done in much the
same manner at the Hippodrome, to say nothing,
about ten years before, in a Princeton Triangle
Club show for which Mr. Herbert Dillon wrote
the accompanying melody, "My Toy Soldier
Love."   No. IV is "Souvenir of the Far Past," the
venerable number out of a score of musical comedies wherein a gray haired old man and a gray
haired old lady slowly and sentimentally dance
one of the old-time dances to the strains of a
wistful tune. No. V is a quartette. No. VI is
an amateurish little vaudeville sketch, the chief
feature of which is a horse with two actors serving as the legs.   It is not in any sense so amusing as the same sort of thing in the Lew Fields
"About Town" act, the Bert Williams "Follies of
1912" act, or the Raymond Hitchcock "Hitchy-
Koo 1920" sketch.   No. VII is, in effect, a crude
version of the beautiful music box number in
John Murray Anderson's revue, "What's in A
Name?"   Other numbers are "Under the Eye of

the Ancestors," substantially a duplication of an act made familiar to Americans in the Marigny revue in Paris in 1913 (in the same revue, incidentally, there was a "Tanagra" scene like the Chauve-Souris' "Porcelaine de Saxe"), some gypsy songs and the familiar "La Grande Opera Italiana" act out of countless vaudeville bills.

What virtues the Chauve-Souris possesses lie in its agreeable air of intimacy, the humours of its compère, the comical Balieff, and its droll manner of staging. The Chauve-Souris of Moscow is an echo of the "Zum Klimperkasten" of the Berlin of the first years of the present century, an echo of the Überbrettl' of the antecedent years—a very, very, very faint echo.

§ 32

L'Accuse.—Looking back over his years of work, a critic finds what is perhaps his greatest amusement in recounting and summing up the accusations that have been made against him and the sinister motives that have been ascribed to him. Personally, after almost two score years in harness, I find that I have been accused of no less than eight hundred odd different critical malpractices, ranging all the way from denouncing a theatrical producer because he had made a sheep's eye at some mythical sweet one on whom I was alleged to be mashed, to writing dispraise of the motion picture as an art because some equally mythical scenarios of my manufacture had been rejected by this or that motion picture company. I have, I find in survey, rarely written a criticism, favourable or unfavourable, that a motive of one sort or another has not been attributed to me.

I make no bumptious boast that I am always truthful. In the first place, I am not ass enough to pretend to know absolutely what the truth is. I merely write what I believe is the truth as I see it, and that I am often wrong I haven't the least doubt. In the second place, it is quite possible that I am sometimes unfair, as all men are sometimes unfair. For I have my prejudices, as have all men, and occasionally they render me anæsthetic to things that other men—some of them idiots and some of them civilized fellows— admire. But otherwise, so far as I am able to understand myself, I have no motive save to report the effect of this or that play, or this or that theory of production, upon the admittedly curious but quite honest bundle of aches that goes by the name signed to my writings. And yet—I have been accused of twice as many crimes against honesty as Wallingford, and of three times as many swindles against integrity as the Right Rev. Dr. Ponzi. Consider the more or less gen-

eral belief that I have in the past deliberately.
opposed the production principles of Mr. David
Belasco because (1) Mr. Belasco turned down a
play that I wrote, (2) declined to send me free
seats to his theatre, (3) assured the late William
Winter that I was an ignoramous, and fit only
for ash-cart driving, (4) attempted to hold the
hand of my mother-in-law, (5) neglected to send
me a Christmas card, (6) never quoted my opinions in the newspaper advertisements, and so on.
The facts are, of course, that none of these things
is even remotely true, save perhaps the third—
and in this regard, had our positions been reversed
and had Mr. Belasco found the prolonged critical
fault with me that I had with him, I doubtless,
being human, would have imparted to Winter the
same news about him.   But surely I understand
men well enough, and have enough humour left in
these old bones, not to hold such a dido against
anyone.   Or consider the not less common assumption that I am skeptical of the motion picture as
a great art because certain of its impresarios have
given scenarios of mine a baleful eye.   The one
and only personal relation that I have ever had
with a motion picture company was the sale of a
chapter out of a book that I had written and published in 1915.   The motion picture company
happened on this chapter (containing a plot for a

play) of its own accord; it had never had word
of any kind about it from me; and it paid for it
promptly and, I thought, very liberally. In addition, contrary to the general rumours, it was
extremely polite in the transaction. I have thus
far never written a scenario and, though God alone
can tell what may happen in the future, probably
never shall. Yet I believe that the movies are no
more an art than the manufacture of merry-go-
rounds.

I have been accused of prejudice against Mr.
J. Hartley Manners because he once complained to
Mr. John Adams Thayer, the owner of the periodical for which I was then writing, of a review I
had written of one of his plays. This is true;
Mr. Manners did complain and, what is more, Mr.
Thayer somewhat sternly brought the complaint to
my attention. But I never pay attention to com-
plaints, unless they seem to me to be sound; and
I paid no more attention to Manners' complaint
than to Thayer's stern observations on that complaint. The only thing that prejudices me against
Mr. Manners, and playwrights like him, is that
his plays seem to me to be in the main very cheap
pieces of box-office writing. I have similarly been
charged with prejudice against Mr. George Broadhurst on the ground that, some years ago, he printed
a pamphlet denouncing me. This not only did

not prejudice me against Broadhurst, but actually
made me unduly friendly toward him. I profit
by denunciation. To be quite frank, it has made
me rich. When my books and the magazines in
which I write are denounced, people buy them.
As my collaborator and I have already pointed
out, when our book, "The American Credo," was
extravagantly praised by the newspapers, it failed
to sell and lost both the publisher and ourselves
considerable boodle. Had it been reviewed un-
favourably and viciously, as most of our books are
reviewed, it would have gone into a second edition
within the first two weeks. I set down only a
few of the prejudices and biases that I am accused
of. They will serve as illustrations. There are
many, many more. But I am actually prejudiced
—and actually have bias—against only three
things. These are sham, cheapness and bad work.

§ 33

The Comic Wits.—Americans returning from
Paris are generally given to a lengthy and admir-
ing recital of the wit of the comiques who stalk
the small stages of the cabarets on the far side
of the river. There are no others like these, they
say, anywhere in the world. Rubbish! I have
listened to every better-grade café concert comedian

that Paris has produced in the last twenty years,
and there isn't one of them one-tenth so witty or
one-twentieth so amusing as the American Will
Rogers.

§ 34

Peacock Alley.—A vain fellow myself, and given
on occasion to an absurd and pestersome roosterish-
ness, it yet beguiles me as a connoisseur of pro-
cacity to meditate from time to time upon the
amour propre of those gentlemen whose profession, if not accomplishment, is the art of acting.
It is a subject that invites. For the actor's vanity
is not a simple thing, founded like mine or yours
upon an easily—nay, almost a childishly—pene-
trable donkeyishness, but one as complex and
majestic as the maze of Amenemhat III. It is not
so much that the actor views himself as a devastat-
ingly pretty one, a holocaust to drive ladies to
drink and servant girls to ruin. There is in this
occasionally warrant for him; for surely there
was not a chambermaid in all of England who
would not have elected a faux pas with George
Alexander to one with Lloyd George or Thomas
Hardy. Nor is there perhaps in our own country
a lady vice crusader or demi-mondaine who would
not fight more tepidly for her honour against Mr.
John Barrymore or Mr. Chauncey Olcott than a-

gainst Warren Gamaliel Harding, or even Bishop
Manning.   There is a flavour even to the beauty
of Mr. George Bickel, I dare say, that is not lost
upon certain fair dilettanti who are stubbornly im-
pervious to the charms of such lesser lights as
Henry Seidel Canby, Joseph Hergesheimer and
Colonel Jacob Ruppert.   No, the vanity of the
actor is not to be challenged on the ground of loveliness, for certainly it would be a brave housewife
who would permit her cook to take the same
chances up a dark alley with a stock company mag-
nifico that she would permit her to take with a
policeman or, indeed, a choir master.

Yet, for all this measure of justification in the
actor's vanity, his chestiness in an ornamental
direction takes on at times an expansion that quite
exceeds the bounds of credulity.   In example, consider the case of Mr. Leo Ditrichstein.   As is well
known, this Ditrichstein has in the last eight or
ten years permitted himself to appear only in such
plays as would vouchsafe him the opportunity to
show himself as a distingué and wistful roué who
irresistibly seduces all the ladies in the cast save
the ingénue, whom he gives over with a magnificently impressive gesture of self-abnegation to
the calf-faced juvenile.   The Ditrichstein vehicles
have come to be so many dramatizations of a
Fatty Arbuckle party, somewhat romanticized by

the injection of white gloves, an Inverness coat and a top hat, several allusions to Claridge's, the Riviera, and Paris under the spring-time moon, a few gilt chairs, a reference to Pol Roger 1906, and the philosophy that it is better to be poor and in love than to be rich and president of the Wiesel Insecticide Company.

Last season, however, the M. Ditrichstein announced that he was done with these revelations of himself as the resplendent and invincible Don Juan, and that he would instead appear in a play in which he would portray a fellow excessively homely and unloved. This, his answer to those who had made sport of his egotism. The play in point was the Italian Sabatino Lopez's "The Ugly Ferrante" and, as one knew from the manuscript, it would treat of the love duel between an inordinately unsightly man on the one side and a remarkably handsome one on the other. And the case against the Ditrichstein vanity seemed to blow up with a loud report. But wait. The opening night. The fiddlers cease. The lights go down. The curtain goes up. And there, upon the stage, sure enough, is our Ditrichstein made up in unornamental red wig and horn spectacles. The jury is about to dismiss the charge. But stop. What is this? The actor who plays the remarkably handsome man comes upon the bühne. Latet

anguis in herba. Ab uno disce omnes. Vanitas
est vanitas. Our Ditrichstein has cunningly cast
for the role of the remarkably handsome creature
an actor with the face of an Hungarian haber-
dasher!

But if the cream of the actor's self-esteem lies
not in the belief in his manly beauty and in its
effect upon the ladies, we find it perhaps in his
assiduous pretensions to intelligence. This is
human enough, and readily understandable. It is
nature for the homely, intelligent man to wish to
be good-looking, and for the good-looking idiot
to wish to be intelligent. Consequently, an actor,
like a pretty flapper, takes infinitely greater pride
in being told that he is intelligent than in being
told that he is handsome. Even the humblest actor
in a barnstorming troupe may be seen while traveling in railway coaches elaborately reading some
book that does not interest him in the least but to
whose content he heroically—and with considerable pseudo-profound conversation—aspires. Of
course, all this effort on the part of the actor is
nonsensical. Intelligence, as I have often observed,
is no more necessary to an actor than good looks
are necessary to a veterinary surgeon. Intelligence
is not an asset to the actor, but something of a
handicap, just as it is a handicap to a clergyman,
a popular song writer or a trousers presser. In-

telligence constipates the emotions, and emotionalism is the actor's sine qua non, as it is the sine
qua non of the evangelist, the composer of popular
songs and others whose prosperity lies in the excitation and capitalization of the simple passions
and ecstasies. Mr. Walter Hampden is an intelligent man and hence the worst of the more
conspicuous Shakespearian actors on our stage.
Yet though intelligence and the profession of acting are correctly divorced, the actor strives preposterously to present himself as a profound fellow, even as does the average stockbroker. This
striving is often jocosely illustrated in the plays
an actor chooses for himself when he sets out on
independent production. There is Mr. Norman
Trevor, for instance. Having played a dozen rôles
in the managers' exhibits wherein he was displayed
as a Romeo, a Brummell and an Adonis, the customary impatience to bask in the light of erudi-
tion seizes this Trevor and, by way of gratifying
his whim, he rushes out and squanders his hard-
earned wages on Fernald's old piece, "The Married
Woman," which has no other virtue than the opportunity it offers the leading actor to be alluded to
by all the other characters as a deep thinker and
to bedevil these characters, when he is on the
stage, with divers magnificent cynicisms.

When the vanity of the actor is not concerned

with his beauty or his intellect, one generally finds
it directed either toward fashionable favour or
managerial achievement. There doubtless never
existed an actor who would not rather be invited
once to tea by Vincent Astor than ten times to
dinner by the President of United States. I may
be doing the estimable Faversham a boorish in-
justice, but if he revived Royle's pifflish "The
Squaw Man" for any other reason than to display
himself in soothing juxtaposition to the smart and
lovely Mrs. Lydig Hoyt I shall be glad publicly
to apologize to him and to pay him libel damages
in the sum of two suggestions as to plays that he
might have much more profitably produced. Further, in the matter of managerial aspiration, consider the effort of the group of actors who styled
themselves the National Repertory Company. It
was the intention of these actors, expressed by
their spokesman in a speech at the première, to
prove to the world for once and all that Erlanger,
Shubert and Hopkins were so many mere office-
boys, and no more necessary to the theatre, the
actor and the drama than the girls who sell chocolates in the rear aisles. The sentiment was
greeted with astounding enthusiasm; the actor
bowed his way to the backdrop full of beaming
confidence in the future; and so loud was the neighing of Cain's storehouse-wagon horses on Saturday

night that the audience thought for a moment that Marilynn Miller's rôle in "Sally" in Erlanger's New Amsterdam Theatre across the street had been taken by General Foch.

These are only a few of the examples of actor vanity lately exposed in the Broadway theatres. In themselves they are trivial, and perhaps not worth chronicling; but there is in them at bottom, for all their triviality, something significant, Of the dramatic productions made in New York last year, no less than twenty-six of the most worthless owed their production, if my confidential agents may be relied upon, directly to the vanity of actors in one form or another. Of these, further, seven more worthy were, by common consent of the professional reviewers and the public, perverted and ruined by the vanity of actors in one form or another. Of these, still further, nine of varying degree of merit were made to suffer a financial loss to their producers by actors' peccadillos generated by vanity of one form or another. And of these, further still, exactly sixteen of the most disastrous from an artistic and commercial point of view would never have been produced had it not been for actors' vanity of this or that sort. Thus, it is perhaps no exaggeration to say that much of the trash that clutters up the native stage is born, and born chiefly, out of the vainglory of the genus mime. One of the leading performers of our stage who recently produced an unspeakable sample of pretentious fustian rejected in its favour a play by Hermann Bahr on the ground that she did not deem it quite nice for her to play the rôle of a woman suspected of infidelity. Another of our leading actors who is announced to appear in a piece by a fifth-rate Broadway hack has, my agents report to me, declined to play in one of the masterpieces of Porto-Riche on the score of its moral quality. A third leading actor, who appeared a year or two ago in one of the conventional Rialto piffles, refused, I am informed, to take the central rôle in an adaptation of one of the truly fine plays of our generation on the ground that it was written by a German and would so hurt his standing in his club. And there is a fourth report to the effect that the production of an excellent drama by one of the best of our native playwrights has been unavoidably held up because of the manager's inability to persuade the most talented of the male stars under his direction to take the rôle of the central character, a passé man whom the heroine rejects in favour of a younger suitor. The list might doubtless be greatly amplified by dramatists and producers. I have set down only a few of the instances that have lately come to my ears.

§ 35

Sheep.—If a Broadway manager happens to score a success with a play in which Ladislaus Zinck makes a million dollars by inventing a non-refillable fountain pen and achieves fame and the hand of the beauteous Gaby Hosenloch by bequeathing his fortune to the Society for the Perpetuation of the Name of Millard H. Fillmore, a half dozen other managers are certain to rush promptly to the fore with plays in which Waldo Püffel makes a million dollars by inventing a non-skid pince-nez and achieves fame and the hand of the beauteous Renée Bierfisch by bequeathing his fortune to the Society for the Perpetuation of the Name of Thomas A. Hendricks. The moment the Messrs. Wagenhals and Kemper began making money on "The Bat," three-fourths of the other managers proceeded to commission the Authors' League of America to dash off plays in which the murder, artfully concealed for two and one-half acts, is finally revealed to have been committed either by the detective himself or by Gundersdorf, the apparently innocent butler, who is actually none other than the evil swami in disguise. The Author's League is still hard at it as I write; and, as a result, when one goes to the theatre these days, the odds are twenty to one that the stage will reveal a corpse shortly after the curtain goes up, and that along about eleven o'clock it will be disclosed that the dirty work was done neither by Fujiyama, the Japanese valet, nor by August P. Wanz, the lawyer, both of whom have been under heavy suspicion because of their shifty manner when the stage is deserted for a moment, but by the actor who is introduced for a few minutes in Act I, and who is kept in his dressing-room by the playwright for the rest of the evening so that the innocentsia out front may be properly surprised and flabbergasted when the dénouement comes.

§ 36

On Action.—Such plays as Gregorio Martinez Sierra's "Cradle Song" are a bit disturbing to those of us writers on the theatre who have devoted ourselves indefatigably to decrying the insistence in the drama upon what is known as action. After many years of commentary in which such commonly spoken of "action" has been made the target of all sorts of ironic and facetious spontoons and djerrids, and in which the complete elimination of such absurd action has been rather obstreperously prayed for, it comes as something of a shock to find one suddenly getting one's wish and being bored half to death as a result.   If ever a

play met the desires of the anti-action school, this
play of Sierra's is it. Placid, reserved, languid,
monotonous, along toward its middle it provokes
in the erstwhile derider of action an ungodly longing for what may be inelegantly described as the
good old Willard Mack stuff. The truth about such
a play is that it is less a play than a short piece of
descriptive fiction incongruously set upon a theatre
stage and peremptorily bid to conduct itself as a
drama. What results is an adroit piece of at-
mospheric writing vocalized by a company of actors
in appropriate costumes, but deficient in all the
elements that go to constitute a theatre play, save
alone colour.

§ 37

De Gustibus.—The dramatic critic of that astounding gazette, the New York *Times*, reviewing
Mr. Arnold Daly's tenancy of the Greenwich Village Theatre, delivered himself as follows: "The
initial bill is made up of two plays. One is a
sombre and Teutonic tragedy of adolescence by the
same Carl Schönherr who wrote 'Thy Name Is
Woman.' The other is a boisterous and entertaining little afterpiece, intended partly to make a
night of it and partly, no doubt, to take the taste
of the former out of the playgoer's mouth."

Now, while it is quite possible that Mr. Daly

designed an obvious little Grand Guignol vaudeville sketch to take the taste of one of the masterpieces of modern European dramatic literature out
of the mouth of the reviewer for the New York
Times, one is privileged to doubt that his intention was any wider in scope. To be sure, about
the only taste that the average New York playgoer
takes to a theatre reposes in his mouth, but, even
so, one must believe that in producing the Schönherr play Mr. Daly viewed it as something serving
a slightly more exalted purpose than a package of
perfumed lozenges. In this, alas, he seems to have
been mistaken. For if this "sombre and Teutonic"
tragedy succeeds only in leaving the New York
theatre critic with a brown tongue and must be relieved by a dose of rough-and-tumble vaudeville,
then in the future we shall have to look after this
type of critic by following up such other sombre
Teutonic tragedies as "The Weavers" with Sophie
Tucker, and such as "Gabriel Schilling's Flight"
with Aunt Jemima and her Jazz Hounds.

Taste is translated by the average American
newspaper theatrical critic in wondrous ways.
Taste, according to this arbiter elegantiarum, is
anything from a musical comedy in which the Emir
does not kick the Grand Vizier in the pantaloons to
a drama in which no one says "Go to hell." In
his category of good taste, this critic lists all drama

that fastidiously avoids life, all comedy that
doesn't venture below the waist-line, and all farce
that is not too uproarious.   Polite piffle he prefers
to stark art.   For to him life is a Methodist butler
in the household of an Eleanor H. Porter, and art
a beggar at the back door.   His world of art has
in it no misery, no bitterness, no blind valour, no
profundity, no sex.   It is an hermaphrodite world
peopled by passions in lovely red neckties.   It is
a world of Pollyannas, Little Nells, Cinderellas
and Little Lord Fauntleroys.   Above it float clouds
with sterling silver linings, and its fields are full
of papier maché posies.   It smells of Jockey Club
and Yang-Llang and Djer-Kiss.   It knows no rains,
no winds, no storms.   It is a sweet monarchy whose
sovereign is the renowned Queen Elizabeth—Lizzie,
for short.

It is this newspaper critical taste in America
that, more than all the commercial managers combined, has retarded American dramatic writing.
It bravely cries for truth and when it gets it either
does not recognize it or seeks to cover its blushful
embarrassment with an evasive eulogy of the star
actor, a couple of redoubtable puns, and a quota-
tion from Dickens.   It roars its encouragement to
a Eugene O'Neill, bids him damn the torpedoes of
hypocrisy and sham and then, when he confounds
it by harking to it and writing a "Diff'rent," takes

quickly to cover. It says to the Theatre Guild:
"Encourage our American playwrights to do fearless and honest work"; and when the Theatre Guild
does so with an "Ambush," it proceeds timorously
to back water and babble irrelevantly and safely
about a "Mr. Pim Passes By." It drives an Avery
Hopwood from the writing of farce that illuminates
the foibles of men and women to the writing of
farce that illuminates only their lingerie. It slaps
itself resolutely upon its manly bosom the while
it cries for Mrs. Winslow's Soothing Syrup. It
demands the naked truth—with a fig-leaf as large
as a rubber plant. It desires comfortable ideas,
comfortable philosophy, comfortable emotions.
It wants life in a Morris chair. . . . The essence
of drama is pain. This essence is bitter to the
American critical tongue.

American dramatic criticism, for all that is said
to the contrary, is not cowardly. That, indeed, is
its leading fault. It is brave in its ignorance,
bold in its amateurishness, fearless in its advance-
ment of the sophomoric point of view. What
American dramatic criticism needs is not boldness,
but cowardice: the cowardice that comes from a
recognition of lack of sophistication, experience,
culture and composite civilization. It needs to be
afraid of expressing unsound opinions, ungrounded
concepts of life and art and letters. If Christ

came to Chicago, He would be not half so greatly
puzzled as if Hauptmann came to New York.

Dramatic criticism in America wears its heart
not upon its sleeve but, more conspicuously, in its
lapel—next to the æsthetic Elk button.   Its calen-
dar year contains three hundred and sixty-five
Valentine Days.   So deeply ingrained is its sentimentality that it is unaware of its presence.   Thus
it praises as devoid of sentimentality some such
play as "A Bill of Divorcement" when the obstreperous sentimentality of the play hits everyone else
between the eyes.   It is still able to detect the
sentimentality in an open and shut Edward Childs
Carpenter play, and to denounce that sentimentality by way of covering up its own Freudian tracks,
but sentimentality masked by the slightest veil takes
it completely off its guard and cruelly betrays
it.   Its sentimentality is so great, indeed, that it
demands it even in its best farces, as witness, for
example, the favourite "Baby Mine" with a heavy
dose of sentimentality injected into the end of Act
I by the producer at the last moment, lest the critical taste otherwise be offended.

The American theatrical producer is keenly privy
to the idiosyncrasies of this critical taste in all of
its ramifications.   A Belasco therefore sagaciously
softens the manuscript hardness of a Laura Mur-
dock by strewing the harlot's bureau top with dolls;

a Gest presents an Aphrodite in a ceinture de chasteté; a Harris proffers the penetrating study of a rotter's character at a matinée with a shrewd show of elaborate misgiving. . . . And the caution of these gentlemen is well taken. For have they not observed that the greatest drama of one of the greatest dramatists of France ("L'Amoureuse") has been denounced by this taste as "cheap clap-trap," that one of the most amusing burlesques of one of the great Englishmen ("Great Catherine") has been dismissed by this taste as "vulgar and indecent"; that one of the best fantastic satirical comedies of one of the most imaginative Hungarians ("Where Ignorance Is Bliss") has been curtly waved aside by this taste as "idiotic, impossible and unintelligible?" They have observed these phenomena, and they have learned their lesson. Why cast pearls, when rhinestones will serve as profitably?

The subtleties of taste are the playthings of the true theatre. With a one-cylinder taste, the theatre can do little in the way of broadening itself and adding to its stature. This, in general, is the position in which the American theatre finds itself today. It is condemned to mince and embroider life, to giggle and fib, to hide behind fans and palm-pots, that it may not challenge the wrath of its critics. Its lungs are cramped, and when it would roar it must remain content merely to whistle. For against it, like the great army of Caesar, is embattled the American critical taste. Which taste, as I have observed, is confined chiefly to the ingestive aperture.

§ 38

The Mystery Play.—The average mystery play fails to mystify for the same reason that the average hotel house-detective fails to detect. One can tell it a mile off. There isn't one hotel house-detective in a hundred who doesn't wear a blue serge suit, black shoes and a black derby hat, and who doesn't spend most of his time leaning against the Western Union telegraph desk in the corner of the lobby. The moment a crook enters a New York hotel, he makes a bee line for the Western Union stand, takes a good long look at the house-detective so that he may know him during his stay at the hotel, and then goes upstairs to steal the diamonds. It is much the same with the mystery plays. The moment the curtain goes up, all the persons in the audience who do not live in Brooklyn pick out the actor in the cast who gets the smallest salary, and then—secure in the knowledge that it was he who killed the man—peacefully devote themselves for the remainder of the evening to reading Beaunash, figuring out the French in the Djer-Kiss advertisement and looking at the girl in the C.-B. corset picture. A mystery play is generally a play in which a murder that puzzles every one on the stage and no one in the audience is solved in a manner that puzzles no one on the stage and every one in the audience. When, at eleven o'clock, Emil S. Gervaise, the great detective, announces that Fitzroy C. Schmidt, the great financier, was murdered by a hypodermic syringe concealed in a Bock panatela sent him by Miguel F. O'Rourke, whose daughter Lakme the financier had ruined, all the other actors are immediately convinced and pair off. The moment Emil opens his hitherto silent mouth and pulls the syringe and the Bock panatela out of his pocket, there is no more doubt on their part; they are fully satisfied as to the solution of the mystery; no vestige of scepticism remains in their minds. The audience, however, isn't always so easily appeased. It occurs to the audience that, despite the sagacious Emil's ratiocinations, there wasn't any Bock panatela in the first act at the time the opulent Fitzroy cashed in, that the fair Lakme was clearly stated to be visiting in Bayonne, N. J., on the day the financier is alleged to have worked his wicked will upon her in Passaic, and that the match with which the deceased tried to light the fatal Bock panatela (provided ihere had

been a Bock panatela) would have gone out anyway.

§ 39

The Viennese Waltz.—I observe that whenever
I take a friend with me to the opening of a new
Viennese musical comedy he invariably, while
pulling on his overcoat, grunts that "this Viennese
waltz thing" is dead and then begins whistling the
tune before he is half-way up the aisle. These
music show Viennese waltzes always remind me of
oyster crackers: one may not care especially for
them but, once they are put in front of one, one
finds them more or less irresistible. The Viennese waltzes are the theatre mood orchestrated.
From Lehar's to Kalmann's and from Fall's to
Eysler's they dramatize the theatre feeling as only
Victor Herbert is able to in this country. They are
tinsel romance and calcium moons and incandes-
cent stars and grease-paint love set to music.

§ 40

The Drama in Springtime.—The moon was shining in the warm, star-shot heavens. The night was
soft and drowsy: a night for music and content-
ment, a night for gin rickeys and laughter, a night

for still country roads and vagrant fancies. And
duty compelled me to go to the Greenwich Village
Theatre to see a play by—Strindberg! Schnitzler, Bahr, Sacha Guitry, Romain Coolus, de Caillavet and de Flers, one of these, perhaps, but
Strindberg! As appropriately put on Ibsen for
a May Day festival, or Björnsterne Björnson as a
cabaret show at Reisenweber's. As well expect
a reviewer to be clear-visioned and reasonable under such circumstances as to invite him to a dress
rehearsal of the "Follies" and then lift the curtain
on "Rosmersholm."

My chief prejudice against Strindberg's "Creditors" lies in the names that the author selected for
his two leading male characters. It is not easy
for me, on a warm, moonlit, springtime evening,
to get very much excited over the love affairs of
men named, respectively, Adolph and Gustav.
The names Adolph and Gustav, however skilful the
dramatist, somehow always recalcitrantly direct my
thoughts to Kolb and Dill and the Rogers Brothers.
When a character named Gustav gets passionate,
I am, alas, reduced to a low snicker. And when
one named Adolph seizes the heroine and hoarsely
bids her fly with him to the Terrazo Superbissimo
at Mentone, I long for the old bar just around the
corner. The name Thekla, with which the illustrious August christened his heroine, is not at all

bad. There is an idea in Thekla, despite its more recent jitney jewel connotation. One may contemplate a Thekla without grinning. Thekla and the Terrazo may not be such a bad combination. But when Thekla is chased around the stage by an amorous Gustav and a concupiscent Adolph, the situation takes on a different face. "Creditors" would be a much more effective play—at least on a moonlit evening in spring—if Strindberg had named his male lovers less after a John J. McNally libretto and more after a Cecil De Mille moving picture.

Perhaps, after all, this whole question of nomenclature is not so ridiculous as I seem to think it is. (Note, in this respect, the extraordinary sagacity of the ear of Shakespeare). The theory that a rose by any other name would smell as sweet is open to challenge. Of this we have ample proof from the experiments in laboratory psychology. Play "The Prisoner of Zenda" exactly as Anthony Hope wrote it, but give the characters Yiddish names, and observe the effect. Or play "Uncle Tom's Cabin" precisely as it was written, merely changing the various names to O'Brien, Fitzpatrick and Murphy, and sit back and listen. Write the finest romantic play you can and christen your hero Sigmund Dinkelblatz, and see what happens. What would have befallen the beauty of Lillian Russell

had her name been Lulu Lachenschnitzl?   And how
much of a matinée idol would John Barrymore remain if he were to change his name to Mischa
Woodel?

It was on another warm, drowsy night of moon
and stars that duty took me by the scruff of
the neck, led me into the Belmont Theatre, and
compelled me to sit through a play by Henri Bernstein, called "La Rafale."   Now, while it may be
true that in springtime a young man's fancy lightly
turns to thoughts of love, it is not true that it turns
to watching the kind of love that such playwrights
as Bernstein trot out on the stage.   Bernstein love,
with its bosom heavings, yellings, grabbings of
the throat and hoofings round the chaise longue,
may be all right for the cold weather, but no one
wants to sit and look at it when the crocuses are up
and when the eiderdown quilt of spring has tucked
away the winter.   On a springtime evening the
spectacle of a fat actress being wooed after a
football coaching system is nothing to persuade
one.   Springtime is the period for the love of "Old
Heidelberg," of "Friends of Our Youth," of "Only
a Dream" and of "The Last Night of Don Juan";
for the love that is lilac or the love that is farcical.
Imagine looking at "Fedora" in the middle of May,
or at "Tosca" in the middle of June.   Imagine being impressed by "Ingomar" when the thermometer

is up and the world outside is full of trembling
lanterns.

I say that duty compelled me to sit through "La
Rafale." I lie. Duty may have compelled me to
sit through the first act and a few minutes of
the second act of "La Rafale," but soon thereafter I looked duty straight in the eye and,
detecting a wink there, bade duty go to. The moon
was still shining and the stars were still twinkling
and the air was still like a warm marshmallow when
I got to the street. Needing more material, I de-
bated to myself as to which theatre should fetch
me. I considered the list. The menu, I concluded, disclosed nothing that was, so to speak, in
season. I pondered the problem. I would go
again to "Shuffle Along"! Now you may say that
any man who would select a negro show on a warm
night is not, for all the probable beauty of his
soul, possessed, strictly speaking, of a particularly
æsthetic nose. And you may be right. But
there is something about this "Shuffle Along,"
whatever its perfumes, that fits with the mood of
springtime. The clogging of coloured feet, the
swing and rhythm of coloured bodies, the wild,
jungle pulsing of coloured tunes—they go better
with the warm moon and warm, windless spring
night than all your intense Gustavs and Adolphs
and Bernstein furours. Sissle and Blake fit the

feeling of spring better than Ibsen and Strindberg, Miller and Lisles better than Hervieu and De Curel. The soft shoe dance is more eloquent than Hauptmann when the moon is on the world, and the Hawaiian quiver immensely more dramatic. All this, of course, such venerable critics as Mr. J. Ranken Towse stoutly and determinedly deny, but when springtime comes no one reads them anyway, so it does not matter. The sober, sound taste of criticism becomes just a trifle wayward, just a trifle mad, when the earth takes off its woolen underwear and puts on its flowered B. V. D.'s. The Strindbergs are for the nights of winter, when the brain is chill. When the robins come sailing back from the southland, bring on the kettle drums and violins, the seltzer siphons and slapsticks, the dancing and the girls! Seriousness, you demand? What could be *more* serious?

§ 41

Dramatic Taste in America.—I quote from the text of the play:

BETTY

(Placing lamp in the window.) You still want this in the window, Maw?

MAW

Always, Betty, every night, dear. *(She sits by the fire-side, takes the big family Bible and opens it.)*

BETTY

Oh, Maw, if our Joe was only here!

MAW

(Stroking Betty's head tenderly.) There, there, Betty! We'll hear from him some day. I know we will. Why, I keep prayin' and prayin' and every time I pray I know the prayer is goin' to be answered.

BETTY

People don't always get what they pray for, Maw. Lots of 'em don't. And you do believe we'll hear from Joe, Maw, honestly?

MAW

I know it. I know it. *(She puts her hand on the Bible, bows her head. The door opens slowly and Joe appears. Betty and Joe stare at each other. The girl does not recognize her brother, whom she had not seen in ten years. Maw turns suddenly and gazes at him. She rises slowly, goes to him and puts her arms about him. Not a word is spoken. The mother's prayer has been answered, as she knew it would be, and when she speaks it is almost in a whisper,)* Joey, my Joey, and you came right in the middle of my prayer!

You say that I am a low jester and have made it up? Or that it is exhumed from some old barn-

storming opus of the James A. Herne period?
Nothing of the kind.   It is from the manuscript of
a play that achieved one of the two greatest successes the American stage of the last six years has
known, a success exceeded only by a play twice as
full of the same sort of stuff. The name of the
play, some of you will recall, is "Turn to the
Right."

§ 42

Degrees of Badness.—However bad any play of
such a writer as Booth Tarkington may be, it is
always better than the correspondingly bad play
of a Broadway playwright.   There is in it a fleet-
ing touch of writing, or of humour, or of observation that is above the reach of the Rialto scrivener.
If a writer like Tarkington is cheap, his is the deliberate cheapness of a man stooping to a plane
of camaraderie with the crowd at a chowder picnic.
The cheapness of the Broadway writers is not deliberate; it is ingrained and unavoidable. The
difference between a bad Broadway play and a bad
Tarkington play is the difference between a bottle
of synthetic New Jersey wine that naturally has
turned sour and a bottle of Cos d'Estournel
whose owner has forgotten to lay it on its
side.

§ 43

Music Show Comedians.—In no department has the American stage improved more than in that of its music show comedians. The music show clown of yesterday was comical chiefly in the degree that he could wiggle his ears without losing his putty nose, or in proportion to the number of steps that he could tumble down without breaking his backbone. There was little subtlety to those fellows of the late 1890's and early 1900's, and one often wonders if such of them as Frank Daniels, Charles Bigelow, Jefferson De Angelis, the Rogers Brothers and Francis Wilson could have earned a living had not someone invented the trick of making a green balloon sprout from a comedian's pate when it was hit with a paddle by Popo, the Imperial Executioner. Without such devices as this, and bereft of ruby coloured waistcoats, baggy topaz trousers and black court-plaster that made it look as if they hadn't any front teeth, the zanies of fifteen and twenty and twenty-five years ago would have been in sore straits. For of the authentic comic spirit they had little, and of a sense of satirical humour, less. Contrasted with this now obsolete school of pantaloon the modern music show comedian is a surprisingly efficient performer, one who is less a clown in the circus sense than a legitimate comic actor. Where, twenty years ago, in order to make an audience laugh a comedian like Jimmie Powers had to put on a red wig, a pair of spacious purple pants, a pair of cardboard ears and then take a running slide across the stage and deject himself with a reverberating bump upon his posterior, a comedian of the present day like Raymond Hitchcock, Al Jolson, Andrew Toombes, Charles Judels, George Bickel or Harry Watson, Jr., is able to extract a three-fold laughter by a wink of the eye, a turn of the hand, a slight ironical cough, or a trick of the voice. Compare Hitchcock's modernized technique, for instance, with that of even such a really amusing fellow of yesterday as Joe Weber. Hitchcock, in his street clothes, can read a laugh into a line by the mere lifting of an eye-brow. Weber, given the same line twenty years ago when it was still comparatively fresh, had to go about dredging the laugh out of it by sticking a sofa pillow under his belt, adorning himself with a pancake derby and a cauliflower boutonnière, and then—after speaking the line—stumbling on a door-mat and bumping his head against the side of the proscenium arch. They earned their wages, did those comedians of another era—but they earned them by means other than true comedy.

These reflections came to me while watching a

revival of "Erminie" with Francis Wilson and De
Wolf Hopper starred in the comedians' rôles.
Wilson is the typical comedian of the ancient
period. His elaborate makeshifts at comedy are
reminiscent of a day when no music show libretto
was considered complete unless it had a Grand
Vizier in its cast of characters, an entrance for
the star comedian atop an elephant, and a topical
song with a last chorus which rhymed the name
of the local mayor with that of the leading local
saloon keeper. He jumps around, slides three
paces to the right, bends in his bustle as if expect-
ing a kick from the rear, gargles elaborately, and
similarly embroiders his lines by way of struggling for the audience's laughter. There is no
ease, no poise, no delicacy. It is all work, and
very hard work. And it is the same, though to
a lesser degree, with his colleague, Hopper. This
Hopper is a comedian superior to Wilson; he, of
the old comiques, has something of the genuine
comic gift; but the flavour of the by-gone days
still clings to him. There is, for all his gifts,
something old-fashioned about him; his kinship
with the "Panjandrum" and "Wang" epoch is
more or less obvious. It is not a matter of lines.
The "Erminie" lines and business, for all their
antiquity, might be made to seem funnier by the
Hitchcock or Ed Wynn or Al Jolson methods than

they are by the passé treatment of Wilson and
Hopper. Jolson can take a jest and a piece
of stage business as old as Chauncey Depew, and
still get an honest chuckle out of it. So can
Wynn; so can Hitchcock; so can a modern imported comedian like G. P. Huntley; so can Bickel,
and Cantor, and a half dozen others who,
like them, either employ the modern comic method
or have adapted their old method to the new requirements. But the old school clowning, as Wilson and Hopper expose it, is wholly empty of
effect, and futile. Watching these men and listening to them seems much like watching and listening
to grandpa tell a funny story. There is a certain agreeable sense of rosemary to the proceedings, but there is no humour.

§ 44

Sacha Guitry.—Sacha Guitry, whom the American theatre has discovered only in the last few
years, is the Schnitzler of the Paris boulevards,
a fellow who, while lacking the Austrian's pene-
tration and sound literary craftsmanship, is yet
like him a witty and charming juggler of the
philosophies of light love. A juggler, unlike
Schnitzler however, who plays more persistently
with cardiac cream-puffs and bon-bons than with

more substantial serio-comic human hearts. Imagine Schnitzler at thirty with a gay flower in his
lapel and eight or nine liqueurs prancing within
him, about to be gathered in by a gendarme similarly tipsy, and you have a more or less accurate
picture of the playwright darling of Paris, as they
call him.

Guitry's plays are by no means plays of the
first rank, and some of them fall far below the
second rank, yet there is none of them that does
not provide a thoroughly winning theatrical evening. From "Wife, Husband and Lover" to
"Father Was Right" and from "The Night Watch-
man" to "Let's Dream" and "I Love You," his
comedies are archly wicked little things of an
admirable theatrical sophistication and worldly
finish. And such of his more sober pieces as
"Pasteur" and "Deburau" are no less graceful
and impressive minor compositions. Like our
own George M. Cohan, he has an instinctive feeling for the theatre, but to this instinctive feeling
he brings a wisdom of the world and a sharp observation of the human parade that bequeath to
his work a measure of body. And the result is
as of a whispered story in a cosy corner, the man
and woman both mildly intoxicated and the front
door locked. His plays are perhaps not for the

soul who seeks "important" plays only and who leaves the theatre moaning when the stage reveals anything other than Shakespeare, Molière or Charles Rann Kennedy, but they are—they are distinctly—for the man who loves a little laugh at life now and then, and who takes his pleasures with his hat at something of a tilt. They are the essence of the Paris of fiction, like the amber lights in the Champs Elysées which, while they do not provide much illumination, are yet sufficiently brilliant and fetching in their little artificial way.

There is a considerable portion of Guitry that is not suited to American digestion. At least, that is what one is told, although why this should be true of a digestion that gleefully massages its middle over "Getting Gertie's Garter," "The Demi-Virgin," "The Sheik," "Jim Jam Jems," "Hot Dog" and other such things, I can't figure out. Much of this forbidden writing is of a rib-shaking humour, fresh, observant and compelling. Nor is it soiled humour, as you may be led to believe. It isn't Sunday School humour, true; yet it is not the cheap, smirking and really dirty humour that the American Avery Hopwood has been manufacturing in the last three years. It is the humour of things eternal, of things essentially and incontrovertibly comic that are yet often held to be

serious.   To delete it from the plays is to remove
the brandy from the peach.   Yet curiously,
enough, it is possible to remove it and leave the
plays still amusing.   This was the case with "Let's
Dream," done in England and America a few
seasons ago as "Sleeping Partners."   For a Guitry
comedy has an overtone that survives absurd adaptation.   I almost believe, indeed, that his "Illusion-
ist" could be adapted for American audiences
with the important last act bedroom episode glossed
over and the play left fully diverting.   Guitry,
in short, seems to me to be the most consistently
droll and interesting young man writing at the present time for the French theatre.   A fellow of literally astonishing versatility, his varied talent has
produced what is perhaps the most jovial satirical
comedy written in France since de Caillavet's
and de Flers' "Le Roi" and the best biographical
drama since Maurice Donnay's "Le Ménage de
Molière," not to mention a number of excellent
farces, a brace of sly librettos. and the most spirited piece of mockery since Lucien Gleize's "Le
Veau d'Or."   There is in him something of the
Hungarians' blithe observation, of the modern
young German comedy school's satirical grasp, of
the delicate drollery of a much multiplied Clare
Kummer, and of the keen dramatic sense of the
best of the Englishmen.

§ 45

For the Defense.—Every now and then some dramatic critic stops momentarily in his effort to compose a story for the *Saturday Evening Post* that will, if accepted, bring him in enough money to pay off the bill at the delicatessen store, to write an article proving that Erlanger and the Shuberts do not know how to run their business. The fact that Erlanger has seventeen Rolls-Royces, nine country houses, and, besides owning a private stock big enough to fill the cellar of the Grand Central Station, is a director of twenty-three banks and sixteen trust companies, and the further fact that the Shuberts are so rich that it takes a staff of one hundred and forty bookkeepers two years to figure out their income tax for one year, do not escape the critic. But this small matter does not restrain him. He nonchalantly waves it aside as he would a mere fly and—he will get at that *Saturday Evening Post* story, he promises the wife, as soon as he finishes this article on the managers —concerns himself with Art.

It is the critic's complaint that Erlanger and the Shuberts (to whom he always bitingly alludes by their first names) and all the other old-line managers are completely anæsthetic to the finer things of the theatre. Art? What do *they* know of Art?

he demands. He is very sarcastic about it. He
even on occasion hints that their religion may
have something to do with their low taste in drama,
and that, if they were true Presbyterians like Butler Davenport, for example, they might produce
great masterpieces like his "The Silent Witness"
instead of the kind of thing they have produced.
But the specific point that the critic desires to
make is this: that Erlanger, the Shuberts and the
other managers like them are valueless to the theatre and drama because they represent the old order of things, because they are of a theatrical
day when commercialism superseded art, because
youth is not only knocking at the door, but already
has its fist halfway through the panel. What the
theatre needs, cries the critic, is this youth. It
needs this youth's spirit of enterprise, æsthetic
integrity, resolution and derring-do. The open
door! The open door!! Give the new manager,
the new producer, a chance. Then, and then only,
will Art triumph over money-bags!

Good enough, so far as it goes. But let us see
what happens when the critic gets his wish. Let
us see what kind of Art the independent newcomer
provides when Erlanger and the Shuberts let
down the portcullis to him. I append a table
showing the Art produced last season by what the
critic calls the New Blood in theatrical produc-

ing: 1. "The Skylark"; 2. "The Mask of Hamlet"; 3. "True to Form"; 4. "Launcelot and Elaine"; 5. "The Man in the Making"; 6. "The Spring" (as produced in the Princess Theatre); 7. "A Bachelor's Night"; 8. "The Great Way"; 9. "Nature's Nobleman"; 10. "Everyday"; 11. "The Fair Circassian"; 12. "Montmartre"; 13. "The Married Woman"; 14. "Desert Sands"; 15. "The First Fifty Years"; 16. A revival of "Trilby"; 17. "The Cat and the Canary"; 18. "Bavu"; 19. "Your Woman and Mine"; 20. "Broken Branches"; 21. "Bronx Express"; 22. "The Night Call"; 23. "The Advertising of Kate"; 24. "The Red Geranium"; 25. "The Rotters"; and 26. "Abie's Irish Rose." Number 27—and it alone—gives the critic support, for number 27 was Daly's independent production of Schönherr's admirable play, "The Children's Tragedy." But roll an eye over the preceding twenty-six. If this is Art, if this is the spirit of the new, independent producer, the revolté, then give us another new show on the Amsterdam Roof and dust off once again the Winter Garden runway!

Surely no one can accuse me of holding a brief either for Mr. Erlanger or Mr. Lee or Mr. J. J. Shubert. For many years Mr. Erlanger barred me from his theatres for the expression of what I believed to be—and still believe to have been—

an honest critical opinion. And the Messrs. Shubert persistently overlook me at Christmas when they send twenty-dollar boxes of Pall Mall cigarettes to my colleagues. But, even so, I am not able to persuade myself that their critical enemies give them a fair deal. They may not be all that one might wish them to be, but what of so many of the other producers and managers who periodically come forward to prove themselves relative paragons? The commercial manager in America is not, and has not been, without his virtues. Despite all of Erlanger's Rolls-Royces and all of the Shuberts' private marble swimming pools, these commercial managers have, with two notable exceptions, produced as many contributions to the art of the theatre and drama as anyone else of their day and time. I need not go in for cataloguing: the theatrical annuals for the last twenty years will give you the necessary evidence. While Erlanger, the Shuberts and the other managers like them may not yet be ready for gold medals, they are surely not the mere targets for custard pies that the critic would have us believe.

I suppose that no man has, in his time, written more—and more acidulously—against the American commercial manager than I have. A lot of it, I believe, has been true, and richly deserved.

But I wonder if some of it—a small part of it, at least—has not been utter nonsense.

§ 46

The Theatrical Year in Paris.—I present herewith a comprehensive chronological catalogue of the most important plays and revues presented in Paris during the theatrical season of 1921-1922, together with the names of the authors and a brief outline of the themes set forth. In the instance of the revues, I set down in brief the nature of the leading features. This catalogue may prove of some value to the professors in our Middle-Western colleges who write in a cosmopolitan manner of the foreign stage, and to the members of the Wentzville, Mo., branch of the Drama League who desire to be au courant with the latest theatrical developments when they visit friends in St. Joe. It provides, in convenient form, a sketchy but nonetheless accurate picture of the contemporary French theatre, and, I believe, fills the want of a people whose familiarity with the subject does not, perhaps, extend much beyond the knowledge that the Comédie Française is situated opposite a particularly good and comparatively cheap restaurant whose specialty is roast beef cooked in the good old American style, and that it is all right for Frenchmen to keep their hats on during the intermissions.

I begin the catalogue with the production of André de la Roche's comedy, *J'Aurais Pu Lui Donner de l'Argent,* in the Théâtre Michel on September 3, 1921, and carry it up through the presentation of Lucien Arête's problem drama, *Lesquels de Vos Souliers Sont Déchirés?* at the Gymnase on the night of June 15, 1922.

Sept. 3. Théâtre Michel. *J'Aurais Pu Lui Donner de l'Argent,* by André de la Roche, dramatic critic of *Le Psaume de la Bohême.* Theme: Gabrielle Heureux, the young country-girl wife of Gaspard Heureux, a wealthy steel manufacturer of advanced years, finds consolation in the embraces of Pierre Fontaine, an impoverished young artist. Her husband, coming into possession of the facts and realizing the difference in the ages of himself and his young wife, provides the means for Pierre to set up an establishment with Gabrielle at Saint Cloud. It is agreed between the two men, however, that this arrangement shall not prevent the husband from visiting his wife occasionally, a compromise to which the young artist agrees only after Gabrielle has confided to him that they need not concern themselves, since Gaspard's inamorata, a danseuse at the Folies Ber-

gère and an intensely jealous creature, is ensconsed
in the chateau adjoining the one that is to be theirs.
The second act passes at Saint Cloud.   Gabrielle and Pierre have tired of each other.   Pierre
has eyes now only for Gaspard's inamorata, who
secretly returns his affection.   They arrange a
rendezvous in the arbour for that night and are surprised by Gabrielle and her husband.   In the end,
all is happy.   Gabrielle returns to her husband's
roof and Pierre and his danseuse are permitted
the use of the spare room.   The play was
a great success, receiving excellent notices from
the playwright-critics of *Le Hanneton, La Gloire,
Le Cochon Animé* and other journals owned by the
publisher of *Le Psaume de la Bohême.*

Sept. 6.   Théâtre Châtelet.   *Madame T. à l'Air
Mécontent,* by Guillaume Mouchoir, dramatic
critic of *Je Suis.*   Theme: Angèle Tendresse, the
young country-girl wife of Henri Tendresse, a
wealthy soap manufacturer of advanced years,
finds consolation in the embraces of Armand Du-
bonnet, an impoverished young sculptor.   Her
husband, coming into possession of the facts
and realizing the difference in the ages of himself and his young wife, provides the means for
Armand to set up an establishment with Angèle
at Versailles.   It is agreed between the two men,

however, that this arrangement shall not prevent
the husband from visiting his wife occasionally,
a compromise to which the young sculptor agrees
only after Angèle has confided to him that they
need not concern themselves, since Henri's belle
amie, a chanteuse at the Ba-Ta-Clan and an intensely jealous creature, is ensconced in the château
adjoining the one that is to be theirs.

The second act passes at Versailles. Angèle
and Armand have tired of each other. Armand
has eyes now only for Henri's belle amie, who
secretly returns his affection. They arrange a
rendezvous in the arbour for that night and are
surprised by Angèle and her husband. In the
end, all is happy. Angèle returns to her husband's roof and Armand and his chanteuse are
installed in the guest room. The play met with
instantaneous favour, receiving enthusiastic notices from the playwright-critics of *Il Est, Nous
Sommes, Elles Sont* and other journals owned by
the publisher of *Je Suis*.

Sept. 8.   Grand Guignol.   Four one-act plays:
La Morte Terrible, by Marcel Déchirant, *La Diph-
thérie*, by Jean Sang, *La Morte Douloureuse*, by
Louis Grondeur, and *La Tuberculeuse*, by Paul
Gaston de Homicide.   Theme of *La Morte Ter-*

rible: A physician finds his wife in a compromising position with his young assistant. While both are asleep, he inoculates them with hydrophobia germs. Theme of *La Diphthérie:* A surgeon finds his wife in a compromising position with a young interne of the hospital. He asks them to smell of a new perfume which, he says, he has just obtained from Algiers. The bottle contains chloroform and, once they are unconscious, he inoculates them with diphtheria germs. Theme of *La Morte Douloureuse:* The scene is a dark cellar, the meeting place of a group of anarchists. One of their number is suspected of being a spy. The others seize and bind him, inoculate him with malaria germs, and fiendishly watch him shiver himself to death. Theme of *La Tuberculeuse:* A woman in the last stages of tuberculosis learns that her boyhood lover is unfaithful to her. She bids him dine with her. After they have risen from the table, she goes to the piano and plays an old love song, a favourite of his. He is turning the leaves of the music for her when, suddenly, she reaches up, crushes her lips to his, and then cries out in demoniacal glee that she has transmitted the disease to him.

Sept. 11. Folies Bergère. A revue entitled, *Eh,*

Bébé!!, by Rire and Sourire. The star, Mlle. Nelly Éclat, in a towering head-dress of four ostrich feathers.

Sept. 12. Jardin de Paris. A revue entitled, *Voilà, Chérie!!!*, by Gaz and Toupie. The star, Mlle. Gaby Rigolade, in a towering head-dress of five ostrich feathers.

Sept. 15. Théâtre des Capucines. *Pour La Patrie*, a patriotic French melodrama by Lucien Brûlant and Max Durchwasser. Theme: Lyse Duchamps has been the wife of François Privas for thirty years. Their one son, Eugène, has grown to manhood and is a captain of artillery. News comes that the Germans have invaded Belgium, are even now outside the gates of Paris. Madame Duchamps, whose great-uncle was an aide of Napoleon's, rushes to the attic to get out the old sword her great-uncle wore at Austerlitz, that Eugène may uphold the proud traditions of the family. Nervously rummaging in the old chest, her hands fall upon a photograph. She hurries to the gas jet to look at it. A cry escapes her lips. It is the photograph of her husband in the uniform of the Potsdam Imperial Huzzars. Her husband is a German! Her son has the blood of the enemy in his veins! She gropes her way blindly down the stairs and finds her husband in the library busily engaged making notes. She demands to know what he is doing. He laughs at her and answers lightly that he is merely making out the family accounts. She regains her composure after a struggle with herself. Slowly, she edges over toward him and glances over his shoulder. On the paper before him are the plans of the Pré Catelan! Her suspicions are verified. Nonchalantly humming a light tune, she steals to her escritoire, covertly removes her great-uncle's revolver, and conceals it in the folds of her dress. She cries out her husband's name, he turns, and she fires a bullet through his heart as, in the street below, the troops march to the front to the stirring strains of the *Marseillaise*. Twenty-nine curtain calls after the second act.

Sept. 18. Théâtre Marigny. A revue entitled *Vive La Paree!!* by Ferdinand Ecrire and P. Gromy. Principals in *Vive La Paree!!*: Harry Pilcer, the Robinson Sisters, Florence Walton, the Original English Pony Ballet, Madge Lessing, the London Trio, Genevieve Williams, Les Brighton Girls, Bessie Clayton, Ward and Foley, trick bicyclists, and Houdini. Musique nouvelle et arrangements de Sigmund Straus et Jack Carroll. Danses réglées par Bert Andrews et Emil Wachs.

Ballets de M. Leo Staats. Costumes de Mme.
Rosenberg, dessinés par Blumenthal. Toilettes
de Fitzpatrick et Wormser. Chapeaux de McFee.
Mise en scène de Nigel Armstrong. Coiffures de
la Maison Kraus. Accessoires et cartonnage de
MM. Cohen, Levé et Garfunkle. Décors de MM.
Entwistle, Mastbaum et Smith.

Sept. 20. Théâtre Athenée. *Monsieur Amasse-
Richesses-Vite Wallingford,* adapted from the
American play of George M. Cohan by Hervé
Bonchose and Gérard Bernaise. Theme: Monsieur Jacques Raoul Wallingford and his friend,
Monsieur Benoit Daw, arrive in the village of
Pittsburgh, Pennsylvania, intent upon swindling
a rich villager, Monsieur Edouard Lamb, and betraying his daughter, Mlle. Mignon Thérèse Lamb.
Mlle. Mignon is the mistress of Monsieur Sacha
Jasper, the owner of the village *hôtel* but suc-
cumbs to Monsieur Wallingford's charms one
night after the latter has played for her Chopin's
berceuse, op. 57. Monsieur Wallingford now
proceeds to defraud his new mistress' father with
a covered carpet tack which he has invented, but
is prevented from doing so through the efforts of
Monsieur Lamb's mistress, prima ballerina of the
Théâtre Astor in New York. The Mlle. Mignon,
outraged at her lover's attempt to beguile her

father, deserts him for his friend, Monsieur Benoit Daw. Monsieur Wallingford accepts the situation philosophically, announces that he will reform and henceforth lead a virtuous life, and settles down in the village with the ballerina, whom he has persuaded to desert Monsieur Lamb, as his mistress.

Sept. 22. Théâtre des Mathurines. *Molière,* a biographical drama in five acts, by Edmond Renard. Theme: The influence of Molière's eighteen affaires on his life and writings.

Sept. 23. Théâtre Porte Saint-Martin. *Corneille,* a biographical drama in six acts, by René Fouillat. Theme: The influence of Corneille's twenty-six affaires on his life and writings.

Sept. 30. Théâtre Sarah Bernhardt. *Le Petit Lord Fauntlercy,* translated into French by Laurent Trifouillon-Schneider, with Madame Sarah Bernhardt in the leading rôle.

(*To Be Continued*)

§ 47

The American Actor.—The American actor has

contrived to bring his profession into disrepute
by virtue of his own disrespect for it. He has
corrupted it, made mock of it, reduced it to an
absurdity. For one actor who is proud of his
profession instead of the immaculateness of the
creases in his trousers; for one actor who treats
his calling seriously instead of as an avenue to
amour with second-rate females; for one actor
who has enough pride in his profession to give
it the best there is in him—for one such there are
a dozen who are at bottom little more than male
mannequins and who view the stage as a mere
platform from which they may display, to silly
fat women and pale, perfumed men, the volup-
tuousness of their charms.

The American actress has, in the main, profited
by all the mistakes that her male confrère has
committed. By hard work, study and determined
purpose, she has made of herself a figure worthy
of critical respect. But the average American
actor appears to sink lower and lower in the æsthetic scale as year pursues year. There was a
day when he was wont to view his work as a life's
work, when he was wont to consecrate all his en-
ergies and all his faith to the glorification of it.
Our stage today still has on it a goodly number
of these worthy fellows. But the mass of other
actors who today parade themselves before us

are of a different cut, vain, strutting, swivel-eyed
half-wits who have no more knowledge of their
trade than so many painted jumping-jacks in
Schwartz's toy window. These are of the class
who are loudest in their Union demands on the
managers. They will have what they want, or
will know the reason why! They will be treated
as artists, or they will shut down the managers'
theatres! Could anything be more grotesque?
Or pathetic? Look over the current scene with a
concrete eye. In a single play on view in New
York as I write this there are three of these clowns
who—to total their deficiencies—mispronounce the
grand sum of twenty-two words and swallow most
of the remainder, who haven't the faintest notion
of the primitive business of fastening on a wig
so that the hair will not show underneath, who
bump into chairs when they walk off on exit cues,
and who give no more indication of knowing what
the play they are appearing in is about than—
the manager himself. The trouble with the average American actor is that he is recruited from
lowly stock given to equally low ambitions. (I
do not essay anything snobbish in this: the lowly
stock is quite all right; it is the lowly outlook on
life that I specifically allude to.) Looking over
fifty American actors presently appearing on the
stage of New York, one finds that but one of these

is a college graduate, and but two so much as
high-school graduates. Three, before they took
to acting, were haberdashers' clerks, eight were
chorus men, one was a corn doctor, six were traveling salesmen, nine were, and are, high in the
councils of the Elks, one was a medicine show
shillaber, one was a soda-water clerk, two were
employed in stockbrokers' offices, one was a laun-
dry wagon driver, one was a hostler, one was a
barber, and two were bookkeepers. The statistics
of the others are not at hand. Surely, save in the
dubious case of genius that will not be downed,
this is a jocose catalogue from which to draw expo-
nents of an art. Small wonder, then, that the
average drama presented to us is acted in
terms of a lynching. In the small space of a
single month, I have witnessed the following phenomena on Broadway: a peafowlish actor who,
cast for a forty-year old character, vainly got
himself up like a lad of twenty-two; a mime in
the rôle of an elegant of the drawing-rooms who
spoke out of the corner of his mouth, and periodically sucked a rear tooth; a young actor in the
rôle of a fellow of blue blood who spoke à
la Surf Avenue, Coney Island, and played his
sentimental love scenes as if he were doing his best
to keep his nose from running; another young
actor who anticipated each of his humorous lines

with a broad grin; a middle-aged pantaloon who
mispronounced three words in a sentence containing seven; an actor in the rôle of an uncouth
crook who desired to show the audience that he
personally was very tony and who used a's as
broad as a French farce; another actor who, at a
tea-table, lifted the cup and saucer simultaneously to his lips; and a juvenile playing a fellow
of breeding who wiped the perspiration born of
the effort off his brow with the back of his hand,
and flipped it onto the carpet. . . .

§ 48

Chronique Scandaleuse.—On a recent Christmas morning the theatrical reviewers of the New
York newspapers received from a conspicuous
producing manager, with his warm holiday wishes
and as a testimonial of his high admiration for
their exceptional talents, three quart bottles of
rare ambrosial liquor.   Two newspaper reviewers,
during the next three weeks, alluded emphatically
to the producing manager in their critiques as
the foremost artist of the American theatre; another melancholiously deplored the hostility that
had been shown the manager and his producing
credo by certain flippant non-newspaper critics;
and still another proved at length and with much

gusto that, in comparison with this producing manager, Mr. Arthur Hopkins (who drinks all the liquor that he can lay his hands on himself) was a mere hansdoodle.

All this eulogy of the producing manager— apparently so sudden and surprising in view of the late perceptible cooling off of his erstwhile worshipers—was, of course, purely a matter of coincidence. I myself, for example, who was overlooked in the pleasant dispensation—beyond all doubt due to sheer oversight during the Yuletide confusion—at about the same time pointed out the manager's increasing taste in production. Blandly to pose myself here, therefore, as the one exceptionally honest and unbribable critic in New York merely on the ground that I happen to have a very large private stock of my own is surely not my intention. If I am honest, it is only because honesty seems to sell my work better than dishonesty would, which is in itself a form of ethical dishonesty. And, as I have pointed out on more than one occasion, to say that I—or any other man—cannot be bribed is utter nonsense. If the producing manager in question, for instance, were to put on a pair of long black whiskers, meet me at midnight up a dark alley and offer me $50,000 to say in print that he was the one and only true artist in the American theatre, I should accept

immediately and, what is more, I should carry
my shame so far as to admit frankly in my article
that I had accepted the bribe for writing what I
did. The trouble with most bribes is that they
are not big enough. If a theatrical producer sent
me three quarts of grog at Christmas, I should
promptly send them back to him and suggest at
least a full case or nothing, just as I should have
returned to the producer of "Tangerine" his Christmas gold-plated pen and lead pencil—had he not
also, doubtless due to the carelessness of his secre-
tary, overlooked me—and hinted delicately for
the solid gold article. I am open to persuasion
at all times, but my trouble seems to be that no
producer believes it. As a consequence I not only
have to buy my own drinks and dinners (and sign
the checks with my own wooden lead pencil) but—
worse still—when a producer espies me in a restaurant and boldly takes it for granted that I
am not snobbish, I have to buy his too. My reputation for unshakable honesty that has thus come to
me is surely not of my own making, and is a
nuisance. I am honest, but so is the superintendent of a poor-house.

But I deviate from the theme. In the two months
preceding the opening of a certain lately produced play, the playwright and his charming actress-wife gave a succession of affaires intimes at

all of which the younger and perhaps more gregarious newspaper reviewers, together with a distinguished newspaper editor, were conspicuous guests. The conversation was very jolly; the playwright's cigarros are noted for the splendour of their bands and their sweet flavour; his actress-wife is reputed to be the greatest Welsh rabbit virtuosa this side of Wales; and gin, pineapple juice and a dash of Fernet Branca make a superb cocktail. The great night of the opening came. One of the young reviewers hailed the playwright's opus, a propaganda play directed against the immorality and danger of jazz dancing, as but a shade less masterly than Hauptmann at his finest, and the playwright's actress-wife, who played the leading rôle in it, as a supreme and breath-taking histrionic artiste. Another, though perhaps not quite so superlative, followed suit. And the distinguished and handsome newspaper editor hinted urbanely to his own reviewer—an older soul who had not been at the parties—that he considered both the playwright and his actress-wife absolutely thoroughbred artists and that he ventured to hope the reviewer was of the same opinion. The reviewer, one noticed in his morning's review of the play and the star, was.

All this eulogy of the playwright and his actress-wife, which did not stop with the first reviews,

was, of course, as in the instance of the producing manager, the purest coincidence. I myself,
for example, who for all my well-known tooth for
Welsh rabbits was not a guest at the happy revels
—unquestionably due to the carelessness of the
mails and the constant going astray of letters—
though I could detect nothing in the playwright's
masterpiece, wrote praise of his wife's performance (I have always been an admirer of her talents). Thus it would be idiotic to infer that I
insinuate that a newspaper reviewer, even though
still in his impressible years, would deliberately
cozen the truth for a cheese pasty prepared by a
smiling and gracious lady.

One now directs the baton to the oboes and
ukeleles. There is a young actress, a relative of
a preterlapsed public figure, whose assiduous adu-
latory tom-tom-ing by a number of the New York
reviewers has for some time been a considerable
mystery to such persons as, not being in the know,
have failed to detect in the young actress' performances any warrant for the excitement. My
own curiosity in the matter mounting, as with each
successive performance the encomiums grew richer,
I presently dispatched my personal coloured detective, the invaluable Mr. Gitz Kraus, Harvard
'08, to conduct an investigation. Although I do
not vouch for the accuracy of the M. Kraus' find-

ings, it appears from his confidential report that
the erstwhile undecipherable eulogy of the young
actress on the part of one newspaper is due to
the fact that she is a god-child of the journal's
directing editor, that the hosannahs of two other
reviewers may or may not be due to the circumstance that the shrewd young actress conducts a
"salon" of which each is, she confides to each of
them, the leading light, and that the horn-blowing
of still another reviewer, a competent but susceptible fellow, has been induced by still another
reviewer who has on occasion acted as the young
lady's paid press-agent. . . .

Walking up the Avenue with Mencken toward
a moonful midnight of several months ago in pursuit of our bi-weekly practice of gazing in admiration at the façade of St. Thomas', it occurred to
us that some diversion might be found in the
literaturklatsch conducted nightly in the nearby
studio of a writer who happens to be a mutual
friend of ours. Among the literati, imbibii and
beauty there assembled, we observed, and were
introduced to, the woman who is without doubt
the most charming of American actresses, a woman
shortly discovered by us to be the possessor
of a genial cynicism, a sharp and piercing humour,
and a talent for sly and lovely flattery that works
upon its victim like Glauber's salt. Gradually,

as the clock moved around to two, the gathering began to break up. The hostess presently retired; Mencken, tired of waiting for me to put on my hat, snoozed off in a large chair; and the subject of this discourse and myself persistently held our ground out in the dining-room over the mineral waters. With the eleventh seidel of mineral water I made bold to ask my fair companion how she had contrived so successfully to win over to a certain critically irrelevant cause which she had lately espoused—and victoriously—several of the young newspaper reviewers. "My dear boy," she beamed at me, and since I am more than forty, gray, and free from rheumatism only in the ears, the "boy" was not lost on me, "what"—and here she again filled my seidel for me—"what would *you* have done in a similar situation after a pleasant evening like this with me?" I answered that my eighteen years in the monastery of St. Sebastien at Monte San Angelo gave me confidence in stating that, despite her beauty, incontrovertible personal persuasiveness and talent for filling my seidel, I should have permitted her to influence me not in the least. . . . At four o'clock in the morning, the mineral water being all gone, I made my adieux. . . . A week later my interesting companion opened in a new play and gave a performance that was a disappointment. . . .

Looking back at my review of her performance,
I observe, however, that I somehow neglected to
mention anything at all of its having been a disappointment and confined myself instead to a
most eloquent tribute to the admirable quality of
her speaking voice and to the hope that we might
some day soon hear it in Shakespeare.

Well, I suppose that we are all human —I no
less than my younger colleagues who admire the
delightful Miss Barrymore—but this is not my
point.   My point is that it is not the business of
a dramatic critic to be human.   And human he
inevitably will be if he is called "my dear boy."
The place of the critic is in the home.   It is impossible for any man, save he be a disgusting
boor, not to be influenced by charming personal
friendships, by invitations to agreeable parties, by
adroitly manœuvered and convincingly propelled
flattery, by gifts of schnapps and fancy lead
pencils, by Corona Superbissimas and cocktails of
gin, pineapple juice and a dash of Fernet Branca.
Some of us are given to the pose that such things
mean absolutely nothing to us, that we are not
so absurdly to be hornswoggled from the path of
duty and the pursuit of truth, but we know in our
hearts that we are lying.   Show me the critic who
can go to a series of parties at a playwright's
house, smoke the playwright's toothsome segars,

drink the playwright's tasty liquor, and eat the playwright's wife's palatable Welsh rabbits—my own invitations, as I have said, doubtless went astray; the mails are getting *very* careless—and then write that the plays of the playwright are the flubdub they actually are, and I shall contribute $10,000 to a bronze statue of the critic to be erected in Times Square. All that I can say is that I could not do it, and I am notoriously an evil-mannered, self-centered and pertinaciously nasty fellow, answerable only to God and the police.

II

But again I digress from the theme. The baton now turns to the accordions and trombones. For several years—until a few months ago—it was a general cause for wonderment and speculation that a New York newspaper reviewer, conspicuously a "moral" critic who could not abide French drama in any form and who denounced the masterpieces of Porto-Riche, De Curel and Donnay out of hand on Methodistic grounds—that this reviewer should regularly praise, or at worst judiciously let down, the naughty plays produced from time to time by the Rev. Dr. A. H. Woods. And this the more so since the reviewer in question was not only not a cigar smoker, but a man who, if humorously susceptible to managerial and auctorial flattery, was yet honest almost to the point of childish obstreperousness. My wayward curiosity being aroused as in the case of the excessive blarney in behalf of the young neo-Duse, I again summoned my private bloodhound, the percipient M. Kraus, and bade him sniff the mystery. After a period of nosing hither and thither, returned the talented M. Kraus with the key to the cipher. Once again I do not vouch for the accuracy of the M. Kraus' report, but present it merely for what it may be worth. This report brought to light the piquant news that the Rev. Dr. Woods, alone of all the New York producers, seemed to be an enthusiastic admirer of certain plays that the wife of the reviewer had composed and that had received a chilly reception in other managerial quarters, had with equal enthusiasm paid the usual advance royalties one one or more of them, and had with even greater enthusiasm promised a production or two as soon as he could surmount the difficulty of getting together a cast sufficiently capable of doing justice to such extraordinary masterpieces.

The case of this reviewer recalls that of another, since retired from active practice, who was even more peculiarly hospitable to the productions of a manager who by no stretch of the imagination could ever have been accused of putting on plays to the reviewer's otherwise fastidious classic taste. It developed that the admiration of this particular lover of Shakespeare for the type of play produced by the manager in point began shortly after the manager bought one of the gentleman's numerous play synopses, and that it increased as the manager bought a second, a third, and even a fourth. This was nine or ten years ago. The plays have never been elaborated and finished, and never produced.

What I here spread upon the minutes is surely not put forth as scandal; my intention is simply to entertain you with some more or less humorous undertones of metropolitan reviewing. As I have said before, it is not my purpose to expose and thus uplift. The world, as I see it, is altogether too good as it is; a few assaults upon its trust and faith with the slapstick of satiric comedy must inevitably be of benefit to it. The notion that a theatre reviewer must be any more honest than, say, a lawyer, or a member of Congress, or an ambassador—each of whom is popularly respected for his talent for being anything but scrupulously honest—this notion eludes me. Why should a reviewer who writes with painstaking honesty that "Nature's Nobleman" is trash be looked on with greater respect and favour than a reviewer who

writes with dubious honesty that it is not trash?
What difference does it make? What conceivable critical and artistic purpose can either reviewer, or either review, serve?   Who cares, save
it be the author and producer of "Nature's Nobleman" who, being the author and producer of "Nature's Nobleman," do not in the least matter? The
reviewer who writes that "Nature's Nobleman" is
trash may hurt trade, but that has nothing to do
with criticism or with art. The reviewer who
writes that "Nature's Nobleman" is not trash
may help trade, but that has no more to do with
criticism or with art. The reviewer's ethical honesty or dishonesty is thus of no moment in any
consideration of the professional practice of æsthetic opinion. Nor has the indubitable fact that
the reviewer who writes that "Nature's Nobleman"
isn't trash is a jackass of the first carat any more
bearing upon the matter. There are two New
York reviewers who have set down their opinion
that Hauptmann's "Weavers" is so much realistic
junk. These opinions were honest opinions.
What, in turn, does it matter?   Would it not have
been better had the two gentlemen been less honest?   Absolutely honest critical opinion on the
part of divers New York newspaper reviewers has,
in the last twelve years, eulogized in terms of
masterpieces such things as Charles Rann Ken-

nedy's "The Army with Banners," George Broadhurst's "Bought and Paid For," John Drink-
water's "Mary Stuart," and Sidney Howard's
"Swords." . . .

As the impertinent and often too cocksure author of "The Critic and the Drama" has pointed
out, honesty is one of the chief besetting defects
of metropolitan newspaper play reviewing. With
perhaps two exceptions, there is not a newspaper
reviewer in New York at the present time who is
not more honest than the newspaper that employs
him. The owner of one of the most important
New York newspapers can be—and has been—
effectively approached from time to time by social
and financial interests; the man he employs as a
play reviewer cannot be. But though these reviewers are honest, they are, some of them, adroitly
to be tricked out of their honesty by various subtle stratagems, a few of which I have herein suggested. I wish to say, and say emphatically, that
the reviewers are in such instances doubtless wholly
unconscious of their having been tricked; and I
wish to say, with equal emphasis, that it is often
surely not the intention of the trickers to trick at
all—certainly no producer is so great a fool as to
believe that a five dollar basket of fruit sent to a
reviewer down with cystalgia will win a favourable review where one is not deserved—but re-

sults are results, and results are what concern us.
The reviewer, though he be as honest as old John
Kelly, is yet human; and if he places his human
nature on the firing line, if he has personal relations, however slight, with those whom he must criticize, that human nature must inevitably sooner
or later rise up on its hind legs to bark at his
integrity. If a theatrical manager sent me a
single small cup of beef broth while I was
miserably ill, I am certain that, were I to accept
it, I should somehow be coloured in my critical attitude toward that manager. I might try hard not
to be, but I know full well that in some little way
—it might be *very* little—I would be prejudiced
in his favour. And, surely, other men are not so
different from me.

III

We turn now to the bassoons and harmonicas,
to the matter of theatrical advertising and its effect upon play reviewers. It is a popular belief
that if a theatrical manager were to produce
"Shenandoah" "in one" with a Yiddish tragedian
in the rôle of General Sheridan and were to take
out half-page advertisements in the newspapers,
there would not be a play reviewer in New York
who would not the next morning hail the production as a great masterpiece, and the producer as

a brother to Reinhardt.   The belief has long since
taken its place in the American Credo, along with
the notion that nicotine is a brownish substance that
stains the teeth and fingers, that one can buy a
Japanese girl from her father for immoral purposes for $2.75, and that the Hon. Arthur James
Balfour is so Machiavellian a diplomat that he
could assemble all the Presidents of the United
States from George Washington down to Harding in
a rathskeller and, by the exercise of his smile alone,
at the end of fifteen minutes easily swindle them
out of Alaska, the Philippines and all the money
in the United States Treasury, and at the end of
twenty, after a jolly handshake, depart with their
watches, loose change, trousers and under-drawers.
Yet for all the vitality of the belief it has small
basis in fact.   Save for one evening and one morning New York newspaper, there is none whose reviewer is instructed directly or indirectly to adjust the tone of his criticisms to the amount of advertising inserted by the producer.   Thus, with the
two exceptions referred to, the average New York
reviewer gives no more thought to the matter of
his paper's advertising revenue than he gives to
the application of electromagnetism as a motive
power, the entomology of Australia, or the drama
of Per Hallström.

But though there is no direct connection between

the tone of criticism and the amount of advertising space, one often observes in the instance of at
least two reviewers noted for their critical timidity
a peculiar and unaccustomed bravado when writing of the productions periodically made by such
newer producers and irregular advertisers as, say,
Mr. Henry Baron, and by such experimental organizations and equally irregular advertisers as,
say, the Players' Assembly. I do not intimate that
this bravado is founded upon dishonesty. I merely
observe that it is a trifle puzzling. Subconsciously,
it may be, the reviewers feel that the many thousands of dollars spent annually for advertising by
Mr. Erlanger, or the Shuberts, or Mr. Dillingham,
although they need not influence critical opinion,
at least deserve a measure of reciprocal politesse
that is not necessary in the case of a little producer who puts on a play only now and then and
whose yearly advertising bill does not run higher
than a few hundreds of dollars. It is possible
that I misjudge the situation. Yet, after watching
it closely for fifteen years and more, I cannot resist a small wink of the eye. The reviewer appreciates—doubtless subconsciously—that he can go
the limit in the case of the little producer without
running any risk of embarrassment from the little producer's indignant visit to his boss, just as he
appreciates—also doubtless subconsciously—that

an equal indignation on the part of a producer whose annual advertising bill was $80,000 or $90,000 would prove rather disquieting. This latter ghost of a thought is ever more or less present in the back of his mind. He may rest perfectly secure in the knowledge that, even were the big advertiser to invade the sanctum of his chief and demand his scalp, his chief would stand by him and shoo the invader out into the cold, but a wish for peace and comfort, the wish, perhaps, of all men over forty, subconsciously pulls him back a trifle with its sweetly irresistible check-rein.

Not long ago the reviewer on a New York morning newspaper, in the course of a review of the attraction then playing there, alluded to the Century Theatre as "a mausoleum." The following day the Messrs. Shubert withdrew from the newspaper their advertising, which ran to a yearly total of $30,000. A few days later the reviewer, backed by his editors and the owners of the paper, began a series of articles attacking the Shuberts and accusing them of everything from the corruption of dramatic art to diabetes. Now, it is reasonable to assume that the newspaper in question cherished this view of the Messrs. Shubert during the period in which it was accepting their 30,000 simoleons and reviewing their productions with more or less sympathy. The newspaper was surely not visited by a divine messenger in a dream the night the Messrs. Shubert withdrew their $30,000 worth of advertising and made suddenly privy to all the things it began forthwith to print against them. If, then, the newspaper knew all these things about the Messrs. Shubert while it was accepting their $30,000 worth of advertising, why did it not, being a newspaper, have its reviewer write them? If it did not know them until the information was vouchsafed it by the angel in the dream, why did it publish them so quickly upon the heels of the withdrawal of the advertising? Once again I affirm with my hand upon my heart and my eyes to the roof of the Singer Building that there may be no connection between the withdrawal of the advertising and the trotting out of the bean-shooter; I merely light a fresh cigar, take a deep puff, lay it down on Waldo Frank's "Rahab," and blow my nose.

Although the reviewing on the majority of New York newspapers is not influenced in the slightest by advertising—the case of the New York *Times'* support of its reviewer in the conflict with the Messrs. Shubert affords an example—one wonders how fair the reviews of a producer's attractions would continue to be were the producer to withdraw all his advertising from a newspaper and yet, with perfect cordiality, invite the reviewer of the news-

paper to pass upon the various plays that he presented. Let us say, for example, that Mr. Arthur
Hopkins concluded for one reason or another to
advertise no longer in this or that New York newspaper. Let us say, further, that he then produced,
in the next six months, a half dozen plays and sent
the newspaper in question the usual seats, requesting it to pass judgment upon them. Would the
newspaper, through its reviewer, treat the productions of Mr. Hopkins exactly as it would have
treated them had he not declined to advertise? I
simply pose the question, and retire again to my
cigar and handkerchief.

The newspaper's obvious answer to all this is
that, since there is nothing that compels it to review Mr. Hopkins' plays, whether he advertises
or does not advertise, it need not review them at
all, whether fairly or unfairly. But like so many
obvious answers, this one is not true. If a newspaper sets itself seriously to criticize drama in any
degree—and three-fourths of the New York newspapers make at least a pretense of such serious
reviewing—it is in duty bound to report and criticize drama whoever the producer may be, and
whether he advertises or not. If a newspaper
takes the liberty of criticizing the productions of
one manager from a level higher than the box-
office, if it professes to view drama as an art and

not as a trade, it cannot discriminate against another manager, advertiser or no advertiser.   Its business is not with managers, but with drama.   It either has a dramatic critical department, or it hasn't one.   It can no more say that it will review the productions at the Booth Theatre and not those at the Plymouth than it can say that it will review the news at one police station but not at another.

IV

The coda approaches.   The bass-drummer, in anticipation, sneaks a chew of tobacco, wipes the perspiration from his brow, and shoots back his right cuff.

The reviewer, as I have said, is—like you and me—only human.   And it is this humanness that, once he permits himself any relations with those whom he must criticize, inevitably plays upon him its sardonic pranks.   One New York reviewer, an honest fellow, writes a book and a series of articles for the *Saturday Evening Post* for a certain producer to sign.   The reviewer makes considerable honest money out of his work for the certain producer.   And his reviews of the certain producer's plays during and for some time after the period of composition are confounded to a degree by the amiability that he obviously feels toward the pro-

ducer—an amiability that you or I would unquestionably similarly feel under the same circumstances. . . . Another reviewer, equally honest,
belongs to a club among whose members are several actors. The actors are pleasant fellows; they
are well-liked by the other members of the club;
the reviewer, while not close friends with them,
meets them at luncheon and dinner occasionally
with the rest of the club members. The actors,
though agreeable in the club, now and then give
very poor performances on the stage. But can the
reviewer denounce them as he would actors who are
not members of his club and who, at luncheon the
next day, would not embarrassingly be found sitting next to him? . . . Still another reviewer
writes a play, sells it to a manager, and has it produced. It is not a bad play, but it fails, and
the manager—not a rich one—loses a deal of
money. The manager five weeks later tries to re-
coup his losses by producing a frank box-office
bumper, a very shoddy piece of dramatic writing.
The reviewer knows perfectly well that the box-
office bumper is awful stuff, but, in view of the
manager's losses on his own play, has he it in his
heart to write the truth? Would you have?
Would I have? We wouldn't—and he hasn't.
And he writes—turn to the files for verification—
that it is a most amusing entertainment, "ingenious,

well written, and thoroughly worth the price charged to get in."

§ 49

Volstead Farce.—The average French farce as adapted for American audiences is a combination of the Seventh Commandment and the Eighteenth Amendment: one-half of one per cent. of adultery. The American theatregoer, it seems, would rather be looked on as a complete mental pee-wee than as one given even for a moment to indorsing immorality. Thus he is free to grant that a young woman may live with a loose bachelor in his apartment for a number of weeks if only she tells the audience wistfully at the final curtain that she is "a good girl" ("Kiki"); that the naughtiest Hollywood movie party never winds up with anything more exciting than a kiss ("The Demi-Virgin"); that a chuck under the chin constitutes the sole statutory ground for divorce in France ("Breakfast in Bed"); and that the haylofts in barns are used chiefly for hay ("Getting Gertie's Garter"). If one were to wait in the lobby after an adapted French farce, take the theatregoer by the lapel as he was passing out, and insist to him that Du Barry was Louis XV's fiancée, that the old Haymarket was a branch of the Y. M. C. A., and that the reason they lynch negroes in Georgia is be-

cause the negroes have an objectionable habit of
playing serenades on guitars under the windows
of white women, the theatregoer would gracefully
poise a toe and imbed it in the exact middle of
the seat of one's trousers. But while he is inside
the theatre, and while the curtain is up, the theatregoer may apparently be told anything of the sort
with perfect security. I have tried to figure the
thing out for many years, and with no great success. If 300,000 Americans revel in "The Sheik,"
if the manufacturers of postcards with naughty
legends thereon report a sale of eight million for
1922, and if the guides in the Rue Cabanais in
Paris have been able to boost their fees for our
native joy hunters no less than nine times in the
last ten years, I can't see why the American persists in regarding his theatre as a Sunday School.
Perhaps my error lies in assuming that he does.
Surely the receipts of "The Demi-Virgin" and
"The Rubicon," to say nothing of "Ladies' Night"
and "Up in Mabel's Room," confound such an
estimate of him.

§ 50

The Puritan Mind and the Theatre.—Professional puritanism becomes an increasingly domi-
nant note in the American social, economic and
artistic symphony. Its manifestations are count-

less, and illuminating. The Board of Aldermen
of the City of Boston passes an ordinance forbid-
ding any young girl to appear on the dramatic
stage in legs bare from the knee down: in Boston,
Hauptmann's little Hannele must wear golf stockings. The moving picture censors of the State
of Pennsylvania refuse to pass any film showing
a woman sewing on baby clothes; it implies a
sex act, they explain. A periodical is suppressed
in New York City because it prints a photographic
reproduction of the sculpture of the great Rodin.
One is prohibited by law from buying a cigarette
in the State of Kansas, or playing solitaire on a
train in the State of Texas, or dressing a wax
dummy in an uncurtained shop-window in certain portions of the State of California. Fifteen
of the greatest books written in the last sixty years
are barred from four out of every five American
public libraries. If one saves a man from drown-
ing and seeks to revive him with a jigger of brandy,
one is subject to arrest and given the alternative
of paying a fine or going to prison. One of the
largest of American religious orders affirms that
going to the theatre to see "Ben Hur" and dancing
the minuet are sins against God Almighty. . . .

It is in its operations against the theatre that
the national professional puritanism exposes itself most amusingly. Of this, as good an instance

as any may be found in certain celebrated reports of the Illinois Vigilance Association, a sister organization to the eminent New York Society for the Suppression of Vice and a typical present-day American institution.   A study of these documents, a dozen or so in number, is profitable in illustration of the lengths to which professional moral crusading has come to carry itself in the last six years.   One of the reports, for example, is devoted to an indignant condemnatory summary of "The Passing Show," a Winter Garden revue produced by the Messrs. Shubert.   Here are a few excerpts:

1. "The costumes are a miscellaneous collection of long and short skirts."
2. "Some of the dancing is done in high-heeled slippers."
3. "Referring to Salome, a muscle dancer, one of the comedians in a dialogue said: 'She used everything but her feet.   Her name ought to be Spearmint, she is so Wrigley.' "
4. "The remark, 'Prohibition is a revenue destroyer,' made a great hit."
5. " 'On the level, you are a devil, but I will make an angel out of you', was the chorus of one of the song hits."
6. "During one of the scenes a little screened cottage is hurriedly built upon the stage.   The ideal home life was pictured in song by the wife and husband, but was ruined by the latter's indulgence in rum.

Staggering up to the door, the husband is answered with a rolling-pin and a miniature trunk, which the wife exasperatingly throws after him. The door is closed with a loud bang, while the drunkard staggers away. Suddenly it opens and a dear little child of three or four years comes out upon the stage calling 'Daddy, Daddy, come here.' The child unites the parents and they dance off the stage with the youngster in their arms. But, oh! What a shameful place for innocent children!"

7. "During the War Stamp Song a number of the girls passed down through the audience selling thrift stamps. The box patrons on the main floor were supplied by girls in white satin pantalettes and vestees trimmed in green, What a shame that our flag, our government and our patriotism all be dragged in the dust this way!"

8. "Often the audience was surprised to see some of the chorus girls sing or whistle from seats in the boxes, main, or balcony floors."

This report bears the caption, "Shall Dramatic Exhibits Be Exploited for Money as Against the Safety and Character of Our Youth?" Picture the kind of mind that reads indecency in a woman's short skirt, in a dance with high-heeled slippers, in such jokes about chewing gum and Prohibition, in a foolish popular sentimental ditty, in the presence of a child upon the stage, in white satin pantalettes and vests trimmed with green, and in a song from a stage box!

"Our recent investigations show that the modern theatrical stage is set for hell," continues a second report. "The stage now reeks with moral filth and sensual exhibits. There must be no discrimination in favour of the costly playhouses where artistic effects and brilliant illumination lend charm and cover the cruder features of the play with an atmosphere of the subtle and the sensual that bewilders and checks the dull conscience of the average person." In illustration of this "atmosphere of the subtle and the sensual," the following is emblazoned in twelve-point Caslon:

"Mr. Cecil Lean, impersonating a happy American sex-novelist, arrives in the play, so to speak, in the nick of time. An amorous Italian has just remarked that his brain is on fire, and Lean enters hurriedly and says that he thought he smelled wood burning."

"The war," therefore concludes the report emphatically, "must be waged *on this whole program of evil!*"

The rest of the Association's direct reports on the theatre are in the main of similar nature: a laborious reading of smut into things which, however cheap and banal, may yet be said to be appproximately as dirty as Louisa M. Alcott. They throw a vivid and revelatory light upon the puritan mind of America, a mind that detects

suggestiveness in a woman's ankle, the débâcle of
the national chastity in a pink silk garter, and a
gross and venomous affront to the American flag
in the sale of a government stamp by a smiling
little girl with pretty legs.

"The public," concludes now a separate docu-
ment devoted to summary and criticism, "wearily
endures these shows of reeking sewers and ill-
smelling catch-basins which the modern show
maker *thinks* the public wants." As examples
of the aforesaid "shows of reeking sewers and ill-
smelling catch-basins which the modern show
maker thinks the public wants" and which the
Association says the public wearily endures are
those (*1*) "in which the crook is made a joke"
(*e. g.* "Get-Rich-Quick Wallingford," which the
public wearily endured for two enormously successful seasons); (*2*) "in which stealing is funny"
(*e. g.* "Turn to the Right," which the public with
an equal weariness endured for three successive
crowded years); (*3*) "in which swearing is
entertaining (*e. g.* "Lightnin'," which the public
of a single city with an even greater weariness
endured for more than two entire, packed seasons); and (*4*) in which drunkenness is a virtue (*e. g.* "The Merry Wives of Windsor" and
"Twelfth Night," which the public has with an

overpowering weariness been enduring since the
sixteenth century).

The puritan mind reminds one of the familiar
coloured post-cards sold in the bye-streets of
Paris which show the picture of a church and
which, when held up to the light, dissolve the
church into a racy boudoir. The puritan mind
is always unconsciously holding itself up to the
light. Between its outward aspect and its inner
self there is ever the betraying piece of isinglass.
One doesn't have to look far for the processes
whereby a mind is thus converted into a negative
constantly exposed to evil thought. Seeing dirt
is an attribute of the uneducated and unculti-
vated mind. A small boy, in the quirk centres
of his uncharted brain, sees dirt in a score of
things that, six or eight years later, seem perfectly
innocent to him. In that period of his youngster-
hood when he is in the middle grades of a primary
school, he sees naughtiness in the photograph of
his naked little baby brother, in words like "adultery" that he has surprisingly encountered in the
dictionary, in the sculptured figure of the woman
atop the drinking fountain in the public square.
These things, a few years later, when his mind
has developed a trifle, make no such impression
upon him. The puritan mind, on the contrary,

is always a mind still in the Fifth Grade state of development. Constantly seeing bawdry, as it does, in the cleanest things, it believes that all other minds are in the same arrested state, and so dances its moron jig to the astonishment and consternation of those other minds.

In the second place, Puritanism is a paying business, just as anti-Puritanism is. If I get paid for writing against Puritanism, some other man gets paid for writing and acting in behalf of it. Puritanism as a profession is today the tenth biggest industry in the United States: its salary list and earning power are thirty-six times as great as those of, say, dental surgery, and its work—being obviously thirty-six times as pleasant and exciting —naturally enlists a thirty-six-fold eager drove of applicants. A haberdashery salesman at Lord and Taylor's gets $32.50 a week. His job is a dull job, and one without repute. As a moralist he can earn $12.25 a week more, with all expenses added; he can the meanwhile have a high time spotting holes in the tights of the girls in the burlesque-show houses; and he presents himself to at least a portion of the community in which he lives as an important and worthy Christian citizen. Where, when he was dispensing haberdashery, no one so much as ever gave him a second thought, his name now appears on the top of

letter paper, his powers of elocution are sought by
Y. M. C. A. lecture managers, and the newspapers
print any letter, however idiotic, that he addresses
to the editor. . . . Nine years ago, a dancing girl
bobbed her hair and became famous. Today, a
man bobs his sense of honour and becomes a famous moral crusader.

In the third place, one finds in the many so-
called anti-vice organizations throughout the country a steadily increasing number of women. This
is easy to understand. The kind of woman who
goes in professionally for vice crusading is very
often of a piece with the peculiar kind of woman
who, the doctors tell us, pays them calls to seek
counsel on certain intimate matters, thus to experience the second-hand sex thrill that proceeds
from the narration of such matters to an alien
masculine ear. The professional lady moralist
may doubtless sometimes be sincere, but nine
times in ten you will find that she is simply a
somewhat passée houri on the hunt for physical
provocatives that she can get, alas, only at
second-hand. She is not content to let the police
raid a dubious hotel—the sound and proper
course—but she must herself go along so as not
to miss anything when Lieutenant O'Toole puts
his shoulder against the door of Room 606 and
smashes it in. She is not satisfied to drag the

sad story out of some poor, misled, God-forsaken
little girl; she must subtly enjoy the experience
of repeating it at the meeting of the directorate,
the latter composed mostly of men. It is not
enough that she detect wrongdoings, quietly report them to the proper authorities, and see to
it that they are quietly punished; she must set them
down in print with not a concupiscent detail overlooked and send them through the United States
mails to any one who asks for them.

Do not think I write of the abstract case. A
few weeks ago I sent to the headquarters of one
of the largest anti-vice societies in the country
for its "literature." I used a disguised name
and an unfamiliar address. There was nothing
that indicated who the person requesting this "literature" might be. It might have been a boy of
twelve, or a girl of twelve, for all the anti-vice
society knew. Yet by return post there came,
among the other pamphlets and circulars, one so
absolutely filthy and indecent that the mere send-
ing it through the mails lays the anti-vice organization in question open to a very heavy fine and
jail sentence. If Mr. Sumner, of the New York
Society for the Suppression of Vice, wishes to do
a good job in putting down traffic in actually immoral literature, let him proceed against this sister
society for the suppression of vice. I have the

records, the evidence, in hand. They are his for
the asking. And it may be well to suggest to
him, and to the United States Postal authorities,
that at the bottom of the lascivious pamphlet to
which I have referred there appears this promising line: "Continued in full report to be published later."

Titles of other pamphlets sent out gratis upon
request by this same anti-vice organization—to
any youngster who can spell out his own name and
write down the street number of the family barn,
since the circular advertising them places no other
qualification upon persons to whom they may be
sent save that they be, as in the jocose old *Police
Gazette* advertisements, "students of social problems"—are: "Don't Take a Chance," "Informa-
tion—Venereal Diseases," "To Girl Friends of
Our Soldiers," "Sex Education," and "Adolescence," the last "especially adapted for youths
of either sex." If, as the organization implies in
one of its pamphlets, a boy may be led to view
robbing a delicatessen store as a jolly pastime
after seeing a moving picture in which the robber
is sent to jail for only a short term, what is there
to prevent the same boy from viewing adultery as
a jolly pastime after he has read a two-page leaf-
let in which the adulterer is vaguely threatened
with an ailment that will send him to the hospital

for only a short term? These pamphlets are not for adults: no adult could conceivably be interested in them. If they are designed for youngsters, what things such youngsters, with their innocent and befuddled little heads, must read into them! . . . Still other booklets, sent out by the same organization—to any one old enough to write his address—at from five cents to one dollar, are: "Life's Problems—For Girls 15 to 18," "Perils of Sex Impulse," "Fighting the Traffic in Young Girls," and "The Sexual Necessity," this last at a modest price of ten cents, stamps acceptable.

Of such stuff and of such principles are the minds that seek to regulate the arts in the United States, that view these arts as so many bordellos, hay-mows, and white slave traps. Of such stuff, the puritan mind that is not content, after someone has kindly obliged with a dollar bill, merely to pull a rabbit out of the silk hat, but must needs thereupon deliver an indignant lecture on the rabbit's deplorably promiscuous sexual activities. Of such stuff, the mind that would convert—and is converting—a once clean and rugged people into a race of lecherous and suspicious blue-noses.

.   .   .   .

PART III

MEN AND WOMEN

§ 1

I often wonder why it is that such a ridiculously small proportion of marriages are happy. Of all the married couples I know more or less intimately, only one may be said to approach, even remotely, to happiness. It is not that the other couples are tired of each other; they are not; to the contrary, they are still much taken with each other. It is not that financial matters have intruded themselves to irritate and worry; this is by no means the case; the couples are in easy circumstances. Nor is it a case of chronic illness, or of trials from children, or of mismating, or of dull routine, or of annoyances from in-laws and other relatives, or of diverse interests, or of incompatability of one sort or another. Of this, I am certain. But unhappy they are none the less. They profess not to be, but it is clearly obvious that they are. Why? Is there something in marriage—something philosophically wrong—that no one thus far has accurately plumbed? There have been hundreds of treatises on the subject, and thousands of epigrams, but it would seem that the head of the nail remains

still unhit. Therefore, with my customary good
nature and high sense of duty to service, I venture to come to the rescue. The great majority
of married folk fail to achieve enduring happiness
for the same profound reason that the great majority of bachelors and spinsters fail to achieve
enduring happiness. Happiness is merely an incident in life, not life itself. To ask of marriage
that it perpetuate happiness is therefore to ask
of the family doctor that he cure one's cold in
the head so magnificently that one will never have
a cold in the head again.

§ 2

A woman is charming in the degree that her
body outdoes her mind in the matter of unsophisti-
cation.

§ 3

When a woman betrays the man who loves her,
it is not the man's love that is outraged, but his
trust in the honour and decency of friendship.
He feels that one in whom he has put faith and
confidence—precisely the same sort of faith and
confidence that he reposes in his closest male
friend—has violated the rules of the game. Love

has nothing, or at best very little, to do with his
injured pride and general soreness. He is disgusted, not over the fact that his sweet one has
done badly by his heart, but over the fact that
one whom he met on equal terms and treated
fairly and squarely has turned Judas on him.

§ 4

Women are engrossing chiefly as colours are
engrossing. The woman I like best is the woman
whose mood and beauty suggest a brilliant spec-
trum, a whirling wheel of surprising and dazzling
hues. When my bachelor years have reached the
frontier of the seventies, I shall buy me a strong
spot-light with a revolving disc of twenty different
shades and colours, and hire an Irishman to play
the contraption against my eyes on the long,
cold, late autumn evenings. And I shall thus get
again, and exactly, most of the grand old thrills
that the girls gave me, back in the perfumed
twenties, in the morning of my life.

§ 5

A man may, or may not, be as old as he feels,
but a far more accurate thermometer of his emotional age or youth is to be had in the women he

looks at. The man whose eyes are for women whom youth has deserted confesses automatically to emotional age. He is afraid of the intolerant and derisive challenge of youth; he seeks lack of conflict, coincidence in despair, faded concord— all the things that the reserve and cowardice of emotional age hold out to him as agreeable. The man whose eyes are for youth in women is still eager for the fray. He may be a consummate idiot, but he is still emotionally young, and young in the spirit of romance and adventure.

§ 6

The enduring love is the love that laughs. The man and woman who can laugh at their love, who can kiss with smiles and embrace with chuckles, will outlast in mutual affection all the throat-lumpy, cow-eyed couples of their acquaintance. Nothing dies so quickly in the heart of the woman as the love that has been orchestrated by the man upon the strings of the tear ducts. Nothing lives on so fresh and ever green as the love with a funny-bone.

§ 7

Above everything else, a natural amiability is the quality most essential to a woman's attractive-

ness. If she isn't by nature pleasantly agreeable,
all her beauty, position, sex appeal, wealth and
wit can avail her nothing in her tête-à-tête with
man. She may be as pretty as Lady Marjorie Manners; she may have the position of a Crown Princess; she may have all the physical magnetism of
the late mistress of Prince Murat; she may be as
rich as an Astor and as witty as a Rip; but if God
has failed to endow her with a sincere and honest
smile she will soon or late—as sure as there's a
devil in hell—lose her quarry to the nearest gracious shop-girl.

§ 8

Love is less great than friendship, and less enduring. Friendship is love purged of the havoc
of emotion by the test of time and the trial of
faith.

§ 9

A woman's advantage over a man lies in a matter of vanities. A woman is vain, and makes no
bones about it. Her vanity is admitted, taken for
granted. A man is equally vain, but seeks to
conceal it. To this effort at concealment a woman is privy. Thus, where a man in the presence
of a woman is confounded by the frank openness

of her vanity, a woman, cognizant of the man's
sham and evasion, and penetrating them, has him
at her mercy.

§ 10

A woman, however much she may be in love, still
always seeks and cherishes the admiration of other
men.   A man, deeply in love, not only does not
want the admiration of other women, but more
often deliberately seeks to avoid it.   Man is more
vain than woman when he is not in love.   But
woman in love finds her former share of vanity
doubled.

§ 11

The doctrine that woman is generally the pur-
suer of man is true, but it is also true that in the
course of the pursuit man generally runs backward.

§ 12

It is one of Nature's protective measures to
present a woman to a man always more or less
in the image of her as she was when he first kissed
her.   Thus, a husband rarely grows conscious of
his wife as an ageing and increasingly homely
woman, but continues to see her more or less as

he saw her during the early years of their acquaintance.   He notices a few changes in her, of course
but in general the woman his eyes observe is
very largely his early sweetheart with mere overtones of maturity.   The same thing holds true in
the case of other girls whom a man has known
and loved; always he continues to regard them
more or less as female Peter Pans.   If Nature did
not exercise this subtle dodge, half the husbands
in the world would murder the women they married, and bachelors would be not one-half so vain
as they are.

§ 13

Man is ineradicably a romantic creature.   It is
absolutely necessary for him to romanticize one
thing or another.   If it isn't a woman, it is a country.   If it isn't a country, it is another man.   If it
isn't some other man whom he engauds with his
worshipping admiration, it is himself.   If it isn't
himself, it is his home-life, or his dog, or the
camaraderie of his club, or his college, or his business, or the girl on the cover of a magazine.
A woman may romanticize a man, but she
usually stops there.   In the matter of the majority of things that a man romanticizes, she is a
cynic.

§ 14

The first thing about a woman that ages is her laugh. The laughter of twenty-three is never the laughter of nineteen. The laughter of thirty, for all the cosmetics in the world, is a laughter with lines and crow's feet. A woman may deftly deceive the approaching years: she may retain the face and figure of the youthful twenties: but her laugh will inevitably betray her. For the music of the laugh of the 'teens is the first thing in a woman that dies.

§ 15

A woman has small use for an excessively witty man. The man who is "the life of the party," the man whose indefatigable conversation and humour keep the ball of gayety rolling, the man who with assiduous quip and pleasantry maintains the jocund spirit of the festive evening—that man is the one who nine times in ten goes home without a girl. Women may not admire numskulls, but their love is in the main for more or less taciturn men.

§ 16

The trivial is, in love, the stupendous. A girl

may continue madly to love a man who neglects
her, hurts her, debases her and beats her, but let
him in a thoughtless moment make a joke on the
size of her feet or allude in a heavily humorous
manner to her taste in hats, and before he is able
to say Jack Robinson she will have made a jump
to the next nearest available beau.

§ 17

The idea that man is incapable of understanding woman has been so successfully cultivated by
women that man in the mass has come to take it
for granted. The propaganda has been carried
to the point where the man who today dares say
that he understands women is set down by his
fellowmen as a posturer, a brag, or a downright
jackass. Women, privy to the facts, conceal their
humorous embarrassment before such a man behind a screen of smiles. Men, not knowing what to
make of him, wave him airily aside, as they would
an allusion to streptococci. He is regarded by
them as not quite nice, although they don't exactly know why.

§ 18

A man, when taken with a woman, seeks to make
her over in accordance with his own standards and

ideals. The more she responds to his sculptor's chisel, the more his admiration for her is augmented. But, presently, when the statue is completed and perfect, the man turns to another slab of uncut marble by way of fresh experiment for his unsatisfied vanity.

§ 19

That woman who begins saying to a man, "I don't think you love me any more," and who reiterates it from time to time, is already beginning to fall out of love with him.

§ 20

The trouble with women is not that one gets tired of them, but that one doesn't. This is the true cause of a man's unhappiness. The popular view is that a man is chronically unable to love a woman long, that he tires of her in due time, and that he is then eager to get rid of her as soon as he can. This is sometimes the case. But more often the opposite is true. He does not get tired of the woman; he continues to like her; he doesn't want to lose her; and his troubles begin.

§ 21

Love is never absolute, entire. In it, though it be as deep as the deepest sea, there is always elbow-room for a bit of a glance at some other man or woman.

§ 22

The commonly held notion that there can be no love where there is no respect wears cap and bells. The greatest loves are sometimes those from which respect is completely absent either on the one side or the other. It may be that there can be no enduring love where there is no respect, but that is another matter.

§ 23

One says that this or that girl is attractive, that there is something about her that magnetizes one. What is this something? Generally, it is something that, however captivating, is intrinsically absurd. For example, one of the girls who is most attractive to me is attractive to me, I find, because when she is asked a question she opens her mouth and takes two short breaths before replying. Another, I find, appeals to me because when one tells her a humorous story she has a habit of looking inquiringly for a moment into one's eyes before laughing. And still another— she is nineteen—beguiles me because, after she has had a single cocktail, she proceeds forthwith to get down upon the floor and turn a somersault. Other fools are just like me. But they don't realize it.

§ 24

When a woman past thirty embraces the man she loves, she embraces all the dreams that she has dreamt and lost irrevocably.

§ 25

It is not that a woman is less sentimental than a man, but that her sentiment comes from the heart, whereas the man's comes from the mind. She is thus not so easily addled by it as he is. She can feel and yet control her feelings. But the man, once the sentiment bee stings him, is like a ship that has lost its rudder. He cannot control his heart; it runs amuck; and the woman, loving yet perspicacious, thereupon cuts another notch in her gun.

§ 26

As year chases year, one continues to marvel at the extraordinary lack of beauty among our fashionable débutantes. In the last half dozen years metropolitan society has disclosed only two girls that one could look at without anguish. There have been some agreeable ones, some with soft and pleasant voices, and some with a delicate taste for colour and costume, but only two of the lot have been even vaguely pretty. One wonders why? I have never been one to believe that beauty springs mainly from the gutter. I have never been one to believe that the tenements are richer in feminine beauty than the Avenue. But as I grow older and less the snob, I begin to speculate, and to compare, and to doubt. There is, I recall, beauty in the riff-raff that finds its way to the stage. There is, I recall, beauty in the riff-raff that finds its way to the counters of the big shops of the city, the telephone switchboards, the cheap dance halls. But there is only this negligible beauty in the higher social stratum. Again, one wonders why.

§ 27

The finest of all religions, west of the Orient,

is the Catholic.   It brings its God closer to earth,
nearer to its people, than any other.   The Methodist God is a vague super-Anthony Comstock; the
Presbyterian God is a vague super-Woodrow Wilson; the Jewish God a vague super-Otto Kahn; the
Catholic God a simple, kindly, forgiving, gener-
ous, beautiful and very gentle and human old man.
My own religion, such as it is, changes with the
turn of the years: it is the religion of the girl I
happen at the time to love.   But when I grow too
old for love, I shall become a member of the great
and gorgeous Church of Rome.

§ 28

Of all the things that may make a woman un-
attractive to men, contentiousness is perhaps the
first.   A woman, however beautiful, becomes in-
stantaneously unalluring if her mood is argumen-
tative and combative.   What a man seeks in a
woman is peace, quiet and agreement, however
idiotic his acts or assertions.   Show him such a
woman, and he is hers.

§ 29

One afternoon not long ago, one of my cronies
called me up and in a hoarse voice bade me not

fail to come to his apartment that evening as he had invited a girl whose beauty and charm, he would wager great odds, would promptly knock me off my feet. Affecting my customary air of boredom not without some difficulty—since the fellow, for all his past false alarms, seemed this time to be genuinely excited over his great discovery—I allowed that I would try to show up. Show up, of course, I did, and promptly on time. And what is more, the girl lived up to the enthusiastic testimonial. She was extremely pretty; she was charming; she was gracious, amiable and easy to talk to. She knew how to play with a liqueur; she knew how to smoke a cigarette; she was privy to the winning tricks of significant silence and broken speech and mistrustful half-smiles. Yet I found myself, not fifteen minutes after I had dumped my hat into the umbrella jardinière, ready to go home. She didn't interest me in the least. She had everything that I like, and yet she made no more impression on me than some dull, fat, old woman might have . . . Why, I don't know, and can't figure out. All men have such experiences. Perhaps they are but proofs of the infinite wisdom and humour of God.

§ 30

The most tragic man I know of is the one who

suffers emotions comparatively late in life: the man, for instance, who falls deeply in love for the first time when he is in his late thirties or middle forties, or the man, say, who becomes a deferred patriot, or blue cynic, or religious zealot or what not in his mature years. The lucky and happy man is he who runs the scale of emotions early in life—in his twenties—and who, when he grows older, is thus able recollectively to sift and assort them, and to keep the ones that are pleasing to him and get rid of the ones that are not. Emotions are the province of youth. When age is emotional, it is ridiculous, as ridiculous as the spectacle of the present-day Sarah Bernhardt mooning over a young stage lover.

§ 31

No woman is more beautiful than her neck.

§ 32

A woman is almost generally subversive of a man's dignity. There is something about a woman —even the noblest and finest—that corrupts in greater or lesser degree the texture of a man's position before the bar of the public. A man will labour for years to achieve a dignity in the eyes of his fellows, and then suddenly along will come a woman who will captivate him and in a jiffy send his dignity glimmering. She need not do a single tangible suspect thing, yet the result is ever the same.

§33

I dislike excessively suave men. They always make me think of the feel of cheap satin.

§ 34

Often when I see the picture of the woman co-respondent in a divorce case, I am struck with the superiority of the wife's looks, and wonder what it was about the dubious siren that persuaded the husband to desert his spouse for her. In the last twelve divorce cases that have figured conspicuously in the newspapers the wife has, with one debatable exception, been considerably more sightly than the other woman . . . This may sound like a futile and trivial paragraph, but I believe that there is a bit of evasive philosophy in it somewhere. I thought for a moment that I had my hands on it, and that I had got hold of the reason, but, though I can feel it crawling around in my head, I cannot quite get it into words.

§ 35

It has been my embarrassing experience, as I suppose it has been the embarrassing experience of many critics, to find that in personal contact bad artists so often turn out to be charming fellows and good artists eminently unpleasant ones. During the last year I have met eleven men whose work I have criticised: seven of whom were incompetents and whom I had critically pummelled without quarter, and the other four of whom were sound artists that I had bathed in the greases of my respect and admiration. When I met the seven incompetents, I found them agreeable and amiable men, interesting to talk with and extremely companionable. When I met the four sound craftsmen, I could scarcely bear them. They were devoid of social grace; they were stupid; they were heavy as lead; they were bores.

§ 36

While it may be true that a woman admires intelligence in a man, what she wants is less a concrete and prolonged demonstration of that intelligence than a simple preliminary guarantee. She may relish intelligence in the man's conversation

for fifteen minutes or so, but thereafter she is willing to take the intelligence for granted and have
pleasant nonsense in its stead. This holds true
of every woman in the world—white or black
—under forty.

§ 37

One always loves the more when one is down
with a sickness. In other words, when one's facul-
ties are weakened. In other words, when one cannot think clearly. In other words, when one is,
in comparison with one's normal self, a hollow-
head.

§ 38

It may not always be true, yet it has been my
experience to find it common, that love and a
precisely conducted household do not often go together. When I see a home meticulously managed,
I generally feel, and learn subsequently, that the
love of the man for the woman and of the woman
for the man has been chilled in the degree that
their house and home have been brought to a point
of machinelike operation. Love and butlers are
not handmaidens. Laughing love and the happiness that comes of it are given to carelessness and

disarray, at least in some measure. Perfect
routine is a stranger to them. No woman who
loves a man deeply, wildly, passionately, has
ever been a perfect housekeeper.

§ 39

Woman's major and helpless handicap under
the newer order of Anglo-Saxon civilization lies in
the quality of the names bequeathed her at the font
of baptism. However beautiful the woman, im-
agine a self-respecting man being able to love her
madly if she be labeled with one of these: Ferne,
Juno, Gwladys, Alys, Mae, Rebecca, Maybelle,
Gussie, Bella, Beulah, Grecia, Charity, Lucrece,
Esme, Geta, Evadne, Iole, Lena, Salome, Manilla,
Mignonette, Jacqueminot, Rhea, Nanci, Parma,
Valli, Oza, Titia, Ola, Veronica, Sadhi, Roxie,
Phanny, Regina, Ruby, or Grayce.

§ 40

A man will tolerate any criticism of himself
from a woman, and pay small attention to it.
What he will not stand is criticism of his friends.
More couples have split upon this point than any
other.

§ 41

It is a sign of man's incontrovertible idiocy that he will like any woman who shows signs of liking him.

§ 42

Procrastination is the thief of love.

§ 43

The common notion that the onion is inimical to romance is discovered, upon investigation and reflection, to be baseless. The countries in which romance most flourishes are without exception the onion-eating—or garlic-eating—countries. Italy, the south of France, the valleys of the Pyrenees, the Austria of Vienna's gayest years, Egypt in the north, Sicily—all were and are hospitable to the tearful tuberose: their swains and maidens alike. Only in Japan, of all the moonlit lands of the heart, is the onion déclassé. And Japan is yearly becoming more and more a cold, platonic, prosaic, money-grubbing country, like the United States, England and Denmark, all onionophobe nations.

§ 44

Returning recently to America on one of the great ocean liners, I spent an hour one afternoon making a round of the decks and noting the literary tastes of my fellow countrymen and countrywomen sprawled in the deck chairs. I counted, in all, fifty-three readers, about evenly divided as to sex. Without a single exception, the men had their eyes glued to trash. With but two exceptions, the women were reading respectable literature.

§ 45

Looking over the pages of my forty years, I find that of all the men I have known there has been but one whom I could trust absolutely and of all the women, only one. A sour record, verily. A lugubrious commentary on the world. But is your record any better?

§ 46

Most engaging of all degrees of woman is the flapper. Mixed in her is the too-strong brandy that is adult woman and the too-weak soda that is child. She is the highball of femininity: the perfectly palatable blend.

§ 47

Woman's greatest victory is achieved by complete surrender. Let a woman surrender completely to a man's moods, thoughts, prejudices, habits of life and derelictions from honour, duty and decency, and he cannot get rid of her, however much he may desire to. He is caught irretrievably and irrevocably in the net of her mercilessly amiable self-denial and abnegation. The smiling eyes of the serpent, glued to his, have him wholly in their insidious power. He may pull and howl all he wants to, but he will find that he can't drown out the approaching doomful strains of the wedding march.

§ 48

The eternal popularity of "Cinderella" has been explained on many grounds and in many ways: that it is human nature to wish to see the abused and humble come into their own and abash those who have looked down upon them; that sympathy for one who sweetly bears indignities in silence is ever profound; that it is the desire of most persons that the meek shall inherit the earth; that—

A score of such thats.

I offer an explanation of the persistent popularity that no one, so far as I know, has yet offered; it seems to me to be, in at least one direction, not without some basis in fact.   It is this: that Cinderella has about her something of the rosemary of all men's youth in that every man's first sweetheart was, like her, a poor girl.

§ 49

One of the most obvious and profitable pieces of commerce in professional writing is a writer's agreeable deprecation of himself, the placing of himself either on a plane with his readers or, more profitably still, on a plane below them. The "holier than thou" note is dangerous: it contributes to unpopularity.   Thus the current spectacle of American letters, an industry second only to the cloak and suit business, is an Alphonse-Gaston pantomime in which the elaborate low bowing of the two parties results in a continuous collision of pates, both auspiciously empty.

§ 50

Other ways may fail, but one can always accurately tell a second-rate man by the quality of his emotions. The laughter and the tears of a second-rate man are divining rods that no university training, social experience, worldly culture, or tailor, can hide.

§ 51

Accurately, we envy a man less for the big things than for the comparatively trivial. We envy a millionaire not for his millions but for his comforts that may be had for mere thousands. We envy a great artist less for his talent and the work it produces than for the kudos these bring to him. Envy, in three cases out of every four, will be found upon analysis to be a marked-down emotion.

§52

The trouble is not, as we are constantly being assured, that the great majority of men are emotional and run their affairs and the dependent affairs of their fellow men emotionally, but that the great majority of men are thoughtful and run their affairs and the dependent affairs of their fellow men in pursuance of the results of that meditation. Complete emotionalism is responsible for not nearly so many direful eventualities as incomplete

thought.   The great masses of men think, but they
think faultily, inaccurately, grotesquely.   Com-
pared with their thinking, the quality of their emotionalism is more often thrice sound, thrice salubrious.   A nation run by pure emotionalism is perhaps not a well-run nation, but it is at least a nation that is run better than one controlled by half-
baked thought . . . Lincoln's heart made him a
great statesman.   Harding's mind has made him a
great clown.

§ 53

The man I particularly detest is the man who
always has a smile on his face, who is always the
hail fellow well met, who is always amiable and
hearty.   He ever impresses me as a dinner composed wholly of pie.   And he has precisely the
same effect upon me.

§ 54

I do not, like most persons, care for old friends.
I find that I tire of them, and of their thoughts
and ways.   I like new friends.   They are more
stimulating, more interesting; they give me greater
zest.   I am, therefore, always ready to drop an
old friend with his old familiar routine for a new
one with his fresh and bracing bounce.

§ 55

The Empress Josephine—caviare to the General.

§ 56

The fact that marriage between older persons—
a man over forty, say, and a woman over thirty-
five—seldom turns out unhappily, or at least endures till death the twain parts, is one of the best
possible proofs, it seems to me, of my long-held
contention that nothing is more greatly inimical to
a happy marriage than a sense of romance.   It is,
of course, possible that romance may also attach to
a marriage between such older persons as I have
alluded to, but the romance in this case, where it
exists at all, exists very largely in terms of present
and retrospect rather than, as in marriages between younger persons, in terms of the present and
the future.   The young man and young woman
regard the altar romantically as a starting-point
—and Time chuckles to himself in the rear pew.
The older man and the older woman, on the other
hand, regard the altar more calmly and dispas-
sionately as a comfortable haven after life's
alternately joyous and trouble-fraught voyage—
and Time may snicker all he cares to, in vain.

Romance is for passionate love; and passionate love has no more enduring place in marriage than the moon has in the broad, hard light of day.

§ 57

The aim of every truly civilized man is to be, and to remain, above the mob. Politics, the heart and foundation of democracy, makes even the truly civilized man necessarily one of the mob. This is why the truly civilized man and democracy can have nothing—or, at best, very little—in common.

§ 58

One of the most irritating habits a man can have is that of repeating in conversation certain pet words or phrases. The man who, during the course of his conversation, frequently repeats some such pet word of his as "proposition" or "fatuous" or "wonderful," or some such pet phrase as "germane to" or "militate against," is less endurable to the average person than the man who has habits ten times worse.

§ 59

It was Richard Le Gallienne, I believe, who

once observed with regret that so many available euphonious and charming Christian names for men and women have been wasted on diseases. For example, where a more agreeable sound than that conveyed by the name Catarrh Carter or Diabetes White. Assuredly no current nomenclature is so soothing to the ear. Erysipelas is a prettier name than Alice or Mable or Grace, surely; just as Tonsilitis is a smarter name than George or Henry or even Montgomery. Which is the more mellifluous: Clara Jones or Pneumonia Jones, Gustave Smith or Appendicitis Smith? Which is the more musical: Susan Jackson or Diphtheria Jackson, Jacob Robinson or Syphilis Robinson?

§ 60

The greatest happiness is that of imminent, but not yet quite realized, achievement. To be about to succeed—that is true happiness. To have succeeded—that is to be in the Pschorr brewery, with Bright's disease.

§ 61

The honeymoon as it is practised in modern civilized countries, might well be called a relic of barbarism had not the barbarians, for all their vulgarities, been too civilized to indulge in it. The grossness underlying the idea of the honeymoon is of an unescapable obviousness. The legal and moral imprimatur, the pretty sentiment, the overtone of romance, the accompanying incidentals of tradition such as rice, old shoes, white ribbons, flowers and the brass band at the depot cannot avail to obscure the intrinsic coarseness of the institution. That this aspect of the honeymoon does not evade even the honeymooners themselves may be appreciated from their invariable desire and effort to escape and hide, although, true enough, the honeymooners may at the moment confuse the actual reason for this desire and effort.

At bottom, the honeymoon is merely a sex orgy conducted in public, an elaborate tournament in amour with an audience always more or less present. Imagine a civilized and well-mannered man and woman taking as boudoir confidantes chauffeurs, baggage men, negro Pullman porters, hotel clerks, bell-boys, chambermaids and several hundred shoe-drummers, smutty old ladies, house detectives and other such hotel fauna.

§ 62

The more highly civilized the man, the more

he admires women who are beneath him. The
more highly civilized the woman, the more she
admires men who are above her.

§ 63

· God is just. He has reserved most of the pret-
tiest legs for homely women.

§ 64

It is possible for a woman, during her lifetime,
to love a number of men, and each for a different
and often diametrically opposed quality. A
man, on the other hand, however many women he
may love, loves each and all of them for the same
quality.

§ 65

They talk of the immorality of jazz; such music,
they say, is vicious, lecherous, demoralizing.
Noise is never vicious, lecherous, demoralizing.
The greatest of all aphrodisiacs is a sustained dead
silence.

§ 66

A man is often perversely comical to his fellow

men in the degree that he is a moral, compliant, shirkless and creditable member of the community. The man with a dozen children is thus ever a jocose and ribald subject, as is the man who respectably marries five or six times. If he is not a professional comedian, like Eddie Foy or De Wolf Hopper, say, he is, in the eyes of his less statutable fellows, yet an amateur zany of no mean parts.

§ 67

Men grow to love the memory of their first sweethearts. Women grow to hate the memory of their first lovers.

§ 68

Do I love you? First tell me the quality of my rival.

§ 69

Women, as a general rule, love men as those men are different from the men who love them.

§ 70

I often wonder if other men experience the same difficulty in finding interesting and durable companions that I do. In all the nineteen years that I have been living in New York, my records show that I have met just three men who have amused and interested me enough to make me wish to prolong the acquaintanceship and have it ripen into friendship. These three men were "comfortable" fellows to me; their tastes were largely my own tastes; their attitudes toward life largely my own; and they were agreeable, honourable, straightforward, humorous, pleasant and likable comrades. Many others I have tried and found wanting. This one, apparently promising, turned out to be sneakingly unfair in his dealings with one or two absolute strangers to me for whom I had respect, and somehow after that I couldn't stomach him. That one, an entertaining fellow, had a habit of spitting out the grains of tobacco that would get into his mouth from a plain-tipped cigarette: he did it constantly while talking: I stood it for three or four months, and then could stand it no longer. I knew that I should be able to stand it—I doubtless had habits just as irritating—but I couldn't. Another man, during a conversation, seemed always on tiptoes to discharge a piece of repartee. While I was speaking I could feel him waiting, breathless and impatient, during every other remark of mine for me to finish so that he could spring his rejoinder.

Still another was too full of approbation: he was
always ready to flatter: he never neglected, when
we met, to tell me something flattering about my
work that he had heard this or that idiot say.   I
got so that I couldn't stand the sight of him.   He
liked everybody, that fellow; nothing, nobody, an-
noyed him.   He was altogether too good-natured.
A fifth man, a cultivated and diverting companion,
had a girl who objected to men smoking in her
presence; she said that it made her ill.   Since he
brought the girl to dinner and supper frequently,
I had to give him up, though I disliked to, for he
was himself an amiable and civilized friend.
And so it has gone with me.   This man, to whom
I had taken an initial liking, was too healthy: always telling me how fit he felt: always slapping
himself on the chest and beaming on his trim condition.   That man, an intelligent and comical fellow, was invariably studiously late for an engage-
ment.   From the lot, only the three I have mentioned remained.   And I wonder how these three
stood me.

§ 71

A woman's greatest love is reserved for that man
whose tastes and manners are most in key, and
whose philosophy and worldly conduct are least in
key, with her own.

§ 72

Of all bores, the greatest is the successful man who affects an elaborate modesty. His heavy effort at ingratiating self-discount and detraction is of a piece with a woman's effort to divert the male eye from her anatomical shortcomings by criticizing similar shortcomings in some other woman. And each stratagem is of equally absurd avail. The successful man who professes a humility and a surprise at other men's flattering estimate of him is generally—if you track down his past—a man cheaply born. The man who is not conscious of his success in the world, and consciously proud of it, and amiably contemptuous of his rivals who have failed, is a bounder in his heart. The aristocrat, whether of blood, or trade, or art, is an aristocrat because he knows that he is one.

PART IV

THE WORLD WE LIVE IN

§ 1

The Fight for Liberty.—In 1775 the American people began their great struggle for liberty. One hundred and forty-eight years later they are still at it.

§ 2

The Professional Diplomat.—International diplomacy very largely defeats itself by reason of its excessive professional quality. One professional diplomat set against another arouses the latter's uneasiness and distrust quite as the latter, in turn, arouses the former's uneasiness and distrust. Like rival guards or tackles on two football lines, each with suave grin sniffs the other, measures him, slants an eye to see that he isn't concealing a slice of brick in his fist and, during the process, takes advantage of opportunity to make certain that the slice of brick in his own fist is carefully screened from his opponent. Each diplomat is trained to be suspicious, to narrow the eye, to smirk, and to oil the tongue. The hope for honest, above-board, constructive international give and take from men so coached is to hope for the downright impossible. What the hope of international peace calls for are not such professional diplomatic super-headwaiters, but simple, honest, unaffected men, of whom there are many in every nation. Had each nation sent to Paris an intelligent non-professional citizen with a cosmopolitan sense of sound, ironic humour in place of the smooth, sour professionals they did send, a lasting understanding and agreement might have been born of their man-to-man meeting. Let to the conclave for world peace Great Britain have sent a man like Bernard Shaw, France one like Anatole France, Germany a Ludwig Thoma and America a George Ade or an E. W. Howe, and we should have found ourselves all better off today. . . . And what is more, tomorrow.

§ 3

The Influence of the Jest.—I have always been of the opinion that the so called comic weeklies exercise a far more positive influence on the life of a community than the so-called serious weeklies. It is the trick of life to conduct itself not after the serious criticisms of itself, but after the humorous. The personal conduct of the average American community is affected more greatly by the *Lifes*,

Pucks and *Judges* than by the *Nations, Freemans*
and *New Republics*. The comic paper jokes about
the loquacity of barbers have contrived to make
barbers, the country over, taciturn. The cartoons
of politicians in loud, checkered suits have made
it impossible for politicians to wear such suits,
however much they may feel like doing so. The
jokes about be-diamonded Jews, clay-pipe smoking
Irishmen and chorus girls with penchants for
broiled lobster have had a similar critical effect:
one rarely sees a Jew any longer with a diamond,
or an Irishman smoking a clay pipe, or a chorus
girl ordering lobster. The jokes have made them
veer self-consciously in directions opposite to their
erstwhile inclinations and tastes. What man, after
twenty-five years of jokes on the subject, still has
the courage to drop a pants-button into the collection plate on Sundays, or to eat a Coney Island
frankfurter secure from the recalcitrant suggestion
of dog meat, or to speak in laudatory terms of his
mother-in-law without feeling a bit sheepish, or to
have a dachshund for a pet, or to admit, without
fear of being laughed at, that he was born in Osh-
kosh, Kalamazoo, Hoboken, Pottstown or Peoria?
What father ever thought of using a hair-brush for
spanking purposes until the comic papers fifteen
years ago popularized the implement? What
showman would ever have thought of using a

negro's head as a profitable baseball target in
summer park concessions if the humorous papers
had not advertised the alleged uniform hardness
of black skulls and made the thing a popular comic
legend? Consider the much mocked flowing tie
that no self-respecting artist dares wear any more,
and the long hair that professional pianists have
been compelled to cut to avoid ridicule, and the
suspicion of dishonesty under which even the most
honest Greek has to labour, and the fact that the
last creditor a man thinks of paying is his tailor,
and the inescapable feeling a man has that all the
old ladies on a summer hotel piazza are whispering
scandal, and the regular defeats of William Jennings Bryan, and the bravery it requires today to
wear long, flowing whiskers. Trivial things, true
enough, but influence is to be measured as accurately in trivial concerns as in considerable.
Name one serious journal that, in minor or important matters, has exercised one-tenth so much influence.

§ 4

A Book on Philosophy and Philosophers.—One
of these days I shall turn my enterprise to a book
on philosophy and philosophers. Its aim will be
to dredge up the state and condition of life, mind,

health, and heart of the great philosophers of history at the time when they conceived and recorded their contributions to the wisdom of the world. This will, I believe, go a long way toward permitting us to get at the bottom of the philosophies in point, to understand them more clearly, and perhaps more amusedly, in the light of their genesis and their development. In other words, to let us penetrate to the provoking causes, the probable *personal* reasons, the psychological corner-stones. For example, what had Schopenhauer's girl done to him just before he sat down to write his essay "On Women"? For example, in what condition were Nietzsche's liver and kidneys, and how many bills did he owe, when he wrote "Also Sprach Zarathustra"? Again, what was the exact relationship of John Stuart Mill and his wife at the time he wrote "The Subjection of Women"? Still again, how much hair was Max Stirner losing when he first conceived "The Ego and His Own"? Still again, what did Kant drink? And yet again, what did Darwin's mother-in-law look like at the time he first thought of his theory of evolution? The idea invites.

§ 5

Anonymous Letters.—I often wonder just what satisfaction is derived by the writers of anonymous insulting letters.　However thin-skinned a man may be, he can't very well be insulted by a person whom he does not know and has never heard of, and of whose existence, name and position he is completely unaware.　However tender one's hide, one can't conceivably be bothered very much by the nose-fingerings of an indiscernible ghost.

§ 6

Essay on Modesty.—The Russian Tsar was a despot; he had to be wiped out.　The Russian Bolsheviki in power today are a menace to the world. The German Kaiser and the Germans under him were military mad; they were a menace to the world; they had to be wiped out.　The Turks are a cruel and sinister people; they have to be got rid of.　The French lead immoral lives.　The English are tricky.　The Japs are wily; they must be watched.　The Spanish are a lazy and worthless lot: look at their King: what a weak chin he has!　The Italians are always ready to sell their services to the highest bidder.　The Greeks are shrewd to the point of dishonesty.　The Argentinians are insincere: they are ungrateful to the United States for past favours.　The rest of the South American countries are like silly children; if the United States doesn't look after them

they will go to the dogs. The Irish are a wild lot,
and half crazy. Austria hasn't a mind of her own;
she is the pawn of Germany and German intrigue.
The Chinese are blind and inert. The Mexicans
are bandits. In short, we are the only just, de-
cent, upright, kindly, sensible and moral people
alive in the world today.

§ 7

On Relative Eminence in the United States.—I
have just put my hand into my pocket and pulled
out a one dollar and a five dollar bill. On the one
dollar bill I see a picture of George Washington.
On the five dollar bill I see a picture of Benjamin
Harrison. I put my hand back into my pocket
and pull out a one cent piece and a half dollar.
On the cent is a profile of Abraham Lincoln. On
the half dollar is a profile of Maxine Elliott.

§ 8

Satire.—Satire is the cosmic castor oil. It is
the accused trying the jury, the primordial monkey
descended from man. It lies deeply imbedded in
the heart of every mortal, as it lies deeply imbedded in Nature itself. A free man votes for laws

to fetter him; a Sultan of Turkey visits a bordello in Paris; one of the profoundest of modern dramas is written by a lunatic; the name of the most foul of the sex diseases is borrowed from an idyllic poem; the ambition of the greatest American novelist is to write moving pictures; the owner of the Albany Night Boat bars from the newsstand on his vessel magazines with pictures of girls in bathing suits. . . .

And five of the six chapels of one of the most famous Episcopal churches in America are built at the expense of wealthy pew holders whose real names are, respectively, something closely resembling Einstein, Schoenberg, Kahlheimer, Morgenstern and Rabinowitz.

§ 9

Virum Cano.—The most accurate gauge of a public is to be had in its heroes. A public is betrayed by its admirations. Divide its hero by twenty-five and the result is an autobiography of the public. Roosevelt thus divided was the American public of his time: its brashness, resolution, impressive showiness, picturesque impudence, shallow ethics and philosophy. Woodrow Wilson thus divided was the American public of his time: its altiloquent buncombe, puritanical hypocrisy, spu-

rious logical processes. Harding is the American
public of today: its pollyanna faith in the sunshine
of tomorrow, its trust in God and Lloyd George,
its relapse from polysyllables that meant nothing
to monosyllables that mean less. The public
changes as it changes its heroes. How can one
better determine the quality of public taste, ambition, intelligence and dreams, for instance, than
by an appraisal of the heroes of its favourite
drama? There is no more revelatory instrument
than applause. When a man claps his hands, he
synchronously gives himself away. Who and what
then, in this light, are the creatures that the American public of today would emulate? The repre-
sentative hero of the popular American play of
today—to answer the question—is a man who substitutes a quick, superficial shrewdness for education and intelligence, who believes that virtue consists in frequent public eulogies of his mother,
whose trust in women, democracy and hair salve is
complete, and who makes love by talking.

§ 10

Authors.—There are two groups of authors:
(*1*) those who, when they have finished writing
a book, consider it excellent, and (2) those who,
when they have finished writing a book, consider

it infernally bad. All first-rate authors belong
to the second group.

§ 11

Pacifists.—There are pacifists in pleasure as
well as pacifists in war. The latter are called
cowards. The former are called leading moral
citizens.

§ 12

American Society.—The most significant appraisal of and commentary on American society is
provided by the *Social Register* of New York City.
Approximately half the names appearing therein
are those of stockbrokers, or the children or
grand-children of stockbrokers. In any society
founded upon aristocracy such a thing would be
impossible. In the Almanachs and Blue Books
of aristocratic and civilized Europe one searches
in vain for the name of a single man whose life
has been spent between a ticker and a black-
board.

§ 13

The American University.—External critics of
the American university—that is, the first-grade
universities of the East, such as Harvard, Yale,

Princeton and Cornell, and even their lesser
brothers like Williams, Dartmouth and Amherst—
make the mistake, it seems to me, of considering
it purely as a hall of unqualified metaphysics when
it is in reality more or less a hall of social metaphysics. The American college is a social institution before it is an institution of learning. This, of course, is always stoutly denied,
yet every man who has gone through such
a university knows the truth of it. It is a finishing
school before it is a laboratory. If the American
university doesn't teach a man wisdom, it at least
teaches him how to loiter through life gracefully,
and how to make the other man do his work for
him, and how to laugh and sing, and how to make
love, and how to remember just a little more romantically than another man, and how to smile
tolerantly and pleasantly at his critics. My own
university gave me no learning, no wisdom; but it
gave me some of these other things, and I am not
sure that they are not as important in this serio-
comic world as the former.

§ 14

Ellis Island, D. C.—In the baggage of three im-
migrants, German, Russian and Polish, who were
recently detained at Ellis Island, there was found

respectively (*1*) a copy of Hauptmann's latest play, (*2*) a novel by Gogol, and (*3*) Paderewski's "Légende No. 2" for pianoforte. The taste of the last three Presidents of the United States has been respectively (*1*) for golf, (*2*) for Keith vaudeville, and (*3*) for Griffith moving pictures.

§ 15

The Individual Normalcy.—One of the things about the American character that I cannot grasp is the pride that the typical citizen of the Republic takes in being what he terms "normal." Plumbing the term, one finds that by it he means one who leads a "regular" life. And plumbing in turn the adjective "regular," we find that by it he means a life devoid of emotions not sanctioned by the Y. M. C. A., of pleasures not endorsed by the Epworth League, of artistic passion and philosophical autonomy, of liberal cosmopolitan point of view and independent spirit. Let us view two groups of sixteen men each: first, a group that is strictly within the proud normal American fold; and secondly a group that, by the same definition, is strictly without it.

In the first group are Josephus Daniels, Calvin Coolidge, William H. Anderson, Frank A. Munsey, Houdini, Herbert Hoover, John D. Rockefeller, Jr.,

Congressman Volstead, Brander Matthews, Liggett and Myers, Paul Elmer More, Charles H. Fletcher, General Peyton C. March, Bert Williams and Warren Gamaliel Harding.

In the second group are William Shakespeare, Richard Wagner, Lord Byron, Anatole France, Jesus Christ, Louis XIV, Marc Antony, Franz Liszt, Friedrich Wilhelm Nietzsche, Napoleon Bonaparte, François Villon, King Edward VII, Frédéric Chopin, Miguel de Saavedra Cervantes, Johann Wolfgang von Goethe and George Washington.

§ 16

Sic Transit Gloria.—In New York, as in no other great city in the world, is one constantly entertained by the spectacle of the sudden inflation and equally sudden collapse of public figures of one sort or another.   Rarely six months go by that some fellow, precipitately ballooned into prominence by assiduous log-rolling, publicity or the pervading numskullery of the herd, does not burst with a report so deafening that school-children for miles 'round are scared out of their wits.   The next day he is heard of no more; his name is forgotten in a week; and in his place another balloon begins to blow up blind to the coming pin-prick.

Consider some of the eulogized magnificoes of late years, each and every one without sound talent or ability, yet each and every one elevated by hocus-pocus of this or that sort to a position of pseudo-importance in New York life: The honest "boy politician" who was elected mayor of New York and proclaimed to be at once Presidential timber and the hope of the nation; the dramatic critic who was looked upon as a Great Authority; the newspaper publisher who was by way of being the American Northcliffe until his newspapers one by one began to get sick; the great magazine genius who is now an office-boy; the illustrious gladiator who got the Divine Call to put Hearst out of business; the profound American dramatist whose plays even the mob began suddenly to laugh at; the celebrated humourist whose following sneaked out by way of the back door overnight; the great moving picture genius who is now a hired man working for real estate promoters; the famous novelist, acclaimed the peer of Flaubert, Zola and Balzac, who is now writing movies; the fearless, public-spirited man, burning with zeal to serve his country, who is now a press-agent writing on space. . . . There are hundreds of them. One and all, they have their little day in court and then, *voila!* —the bone-yard.

§ 17

On Medals and Awards of Honour.—As we hurry through life, let us recall that Lea and Perrins have just as many pretty medals as General Pershing, and Crosse and Blackwell three times as many as General Ferdinand Foch.

§ 18

The Question of Freedom.—A man talks a great deal of his love and desire for perfect freedom, yet the truth is that he actually cares much less for perfect freedom than he believes. Given perfect freedom, he would still continue volitionally to impose upon himself most of the physical and mental restrictions that he does at present. It is a rare man who enjoys an absolutely untrammeled existence. Almost every man is a willing slave to those emotions, thoughts, conventions and personal habits that in combination stake out the boundary lines of his freedom. The greatest foe of freedom is man's own nature. He does not want absolute autonomy; he wants, in at least some degree, to be ruled and protected—if not by a king, by a woman; if not by a woman, by his traditional and satisfactory comforts; if not by

his traditional and satisfactory comforts, by the
love or fear of God.

§ 19

There Lies Glamour; There Lay Romance.—
The Malecon at two o'clock of a late Spring morning, with its tiara of amber lights, the harbour
of Havana playing its soft lullaby against the
sea-wall, and Morro Castle blinking like a patient
owl across the waters; the garden of the Hotel
de France et l'Angleterre at Fontainebleau in the
twilight, with the cannon of the French artillery in
late summer manœuvres echoing dully in the out-
lying forests; Hampton Court on a lazy afternoon
in the late autumn of the year, deserted, still,
with the leaves falling across the withered flower-
beds and, up from the Thames, the sound of a
lonely paddle; mid-winter dawn in the Siegesalle
of Berlin; the steps of the Tcheragan Serai in
Constantinople on a moonlit night trembling in
the mirror of the Bosporus; the palm-bordered
road out of Hamilton, Bermuda, on a rainy day in
May, with the smell of the sea dripping from the
great leaves; the hurricane deck of a ship gliding
noiselessly through the blue, star-shot cyclorama of
a Caribbean night, with the intermittent click of
poker chips from the smoking-room and the orch-

estra below playing the waltz song from "Sari";
the Kärntner-Ring of Vienna just after eleven of
a November evening, with its elaborately costumed
police, and the hackmen bawling for fares, and
the young girls selling Kaiserblumen, and the
crowds in dominoes of a dozen colours on their
way to the flower ball, and cavalrymen kissing
their sweethearts in the middle of the street; the
path of pines that winds up the hill on the far side
of Lake Mohegan, its carpet of moss still damp
from the retreat of April, an hour from Times
Square. . . .

§ 20

The Success of Democracy.—The latest available statistics show that the United States employs,
in proportion to the number of its citizens, more
policemen than any other country in the civilized
world.

§ 21

On French Cooking.—One of the most overes-
timated things on this footstool is French cooking.
There are, in Paris, only three restaurants where
the food is unusually toothsome, and the chef of
one of these is a Swiss, and the chef of another
an Alsatian whose blood is two-thirds German.

The French know how to cook certain kinds of fish
better than any other people in the world, but
name a single meat that they can cook so well as
the Germans, a fowl that they can cook so well
as an American negro, a vegetable that they can
toy with so jauntily as the Austrians, a piece of
pastry that they can manufacture so well as the
Danes, or hors d'oeuvres that they can arrange
so tastily as the Swedes. As for soups, the Italians have them completely at sea, as the Turks
have them beaten in the matter of desserts and
coffee, and the English in the matter of cooked
cheese dishes.

§ 22

The First Step.—To abolish war, first abolish
all the brass bands and coloured bunting.

§ 23

Modern advertising.—It often occurs to me
to speculate on the men who are entrusted with
the job of writing and editing the advertisements
of the large American commercial organizations.
In looking through these advertisements in the
magazines and newspapers, I am given pause by
the considerable amount of nonsense incorporated

in them. I frequently wonder if the company officials themselves ever read their own advertisements. For example, in the current large advertisements of the Victor Talking Machine Company, setting forth the virtues of the Victrola, I find this line conspicuously featured: "Public approval follows artistic leadership." What could be more senseless? Public approval generally does nothing of the sort, and nine persons out of ten who read the advertisement are aware of the fact. Again, in an advertisement of the Seth Thomas Clock Company, I note the following: "In 1813 the United States was at war to maintain the principles established by the Revolution. In that period men and purposes passed through the furnace. Genuineness alone survived." Here, more bosh. If genuineness of purpose alone survived the war of 1812—from the Seth Thomas Clock Company's point of view— what, the reader may inquire of the Seth Thomas Clock Company, happened to England? The reader is unaware that anything happened.

"In industry, art, science, good results require good implements kept in good condition," reads the advertisement of the American Telephone and Telegraph Company. Still more nonsense. Arnold Bennett wrote "The Old Wives' Tale" with the only miserable pens that he could find in a

little town in France. The story of Fulton and
his wretched implements is known to every reader
of the Telephone Company's advertisement.
There are hundreds of other examples. We turn
from this advertisement to that of Stephen F.
Whitman and Son. Here we find: "Care in select-
ing the proper package of Whitman's chocolates
to fit the occasion wins golden opinions." This
is enough to make any advertisement reader above
the grade of moron laugh. Consider the phrase
"golden opinions." Consider, further, the be-
stowal of "golden opinions" upon a person because
that person is gifted with the amazing and esoteric
genius for discriminating between chocolate drops
with cream in them and chocolate drops with nuts
in them.

The advertisement of the Pratt and Lambert
Varnish Products Company begins thus:

"Betsy, you'll ruin me yet! When did you buy that
desk?"

"Why, Tommy Boy, that's the little old desk Mother
gave us when we started housekeeping. I just gave it
two coats of Gray Vitralite."

Illustrating this fetching dialogue is a drawing
of a prosperous couple immaculately dressed, the
man in particular. The illustration showing the

article of furniture that would ruin the man is the sort of desk that may be purchased from any Sixth Avenue dealer for about twenty dollars.

The Pepsodent Dentifrice Company's advertisement offers a ten-day trial tube of tooth paste and goes on to announce that "Millions of people have accepted this free offer—have made this ten-day test." In other words, the advertisement asks its reader to believe that at least one person out of every one hundred in the United States has sent in the attached coupon for the free tube of Pepsodent tooth varnish. What reader will for a moment believe such extravagant statistics?

I have picked these advertisements not from this journal and that, carefully and shrewdly to prove my point, but haphazardly from the pages of the periodical that happens to be closest at hand. There are any number of other advertisements in it that reveal a similar dosage of moonshine. In fact, the one and only well-constructed and convincing advertisement in the whole magazine is that of the Pierce-Arrow Motor Car Company. It consists simply of a clear picture reproduction of the automobile with the words "Pierce-Arrow, 7 Passenger" printed beneath it.

§ 24

Aristocracy.—In Europe, aristocracy is founded upon land.   In the United States, it is founded upon real estate.

§ 25

The War with Japan.—They say that there must be no war with Japan, for the Japanese are a thrifty, hard-working, home-loving, studious and progressive people.   In July, 1914, they were still describing the Germans with exactly the same adjectives.

§ 26

Portrait of an American.—A lover of strong liquor and rare wines, a gay Lothario with ever an eye for a pretty girl, white or black, a believer in aristocracy and slavery, a hater of the mob, a gourmet, a virtuoso of Rabelaisianism and amour, the life of the party, a good dancer, a fellow of finical taste in clothes, an admirer of fine art with no regard to its morals. . . . You smile at the viciously satirical picture?   I give you its name: The Father of His Country, George Washington.

§ 27

Government Ownership.—One of the most convincing arguments for government ownership that I have encountered is the Hotel Washington in the Panama Canal Zone. Operated by the United States Government, it is—with the possible exceptions of the Adlon in Berlin and the Roche-Noir at Trouville—the most perfectly managed hotel in the world. It is beautiful; it is unostentatious; it is as quiet as one's own home; it is scrupulously clean; it is inexpensive. The service is prompt and extremely courteous; the irritating atmosphere of the usual hotel is completely absent; the servants have been trained not to keep their hands constantly tipward; the air is that of a large and agreeable country club. The great windows of the rooms to the front of the hotel swing outward to the palm-fronted sea—the most beautiful prospect revealed by any window that I have ever looked through. To the rear is a great palm court circled by wide, white verandas. The halls and corridors of the building are broad and tropically still. (The servants do their work almost unseen.) The dining halls cover a city block; they are extremely simple in design—high and cool green—and extremely lovely; and the food is as good as any you will find the world over. You can't get a drink— it being American territory—but you may bring your bottle to the table and they'll serve it for you without mock secrecy or whispering ado. The United States Government may not be able to run a railroad, but it seems to know more about run‹ ning a hotel than all the other bonifaces in the country combined.

§ 28

The Yokel Soul.—What yokel souls, after all, the most of us have. Take me, for example. I have traveled and lived the world over since boy-hood, and what of all the great grandeur and beauty of foreign lands lingers most persistently (and honestly) in my mind? That the shoe-shines in Berlin are the glossiest I have ever seen; that a sharp pebble got into my shoe while I was looking at the Sphinx and cut my foot; that I lost my hat in Shanghai and couldn't get another to fit me; that I fell off a tally-ho on the way to the Derby and bruised my knee; that I kissed a French girl in the tunnel near Paris on the way from Calais and got my face slapped; that I was arrested in Florence for trying to steal a small tombstone from a grave-yard; that I once discovered an excellent glass of Culmbacher in

Constantinople; that the worst stomach-ache I ever had was during a stay in the Engadine; that while skating in St. Petersburg I once bumped into a fat woman, upset her, and caused her to fracture two ribs; that the best soup I ever tasted was that I got in Stockholm; that I met a native girl in Tokio who took me for a Japanese; that the worst Scotch whiskey I ever drank was some I got in Edinburgh; that I once had my hair cut in Budapest and looked like a freak for a month afterward; that on the wall of my hotel room in Johannesburg there hung a picture of Della Fox; that I had a devil of a time getting a tooth pulled in Tunis . . .

§ 29

The Great Southern Sport.—Whatever else may be charged against the South, it must be admitted that that region has perfected the most engrossing form of sport yet devised by the nimble and ingenious American mind.   I allude, obviously, to Ku Klux Klan-ing.   To believe that the hundred and one Klux organizations currently enjoying themselves south of the Mason-Dixon line are concerned with the dull and extrinsic business of improving the morals and ethical standards of their fellow citizens is to believe that the baseball nines in the National League are concerned with the work of the Church Federation and the Salvation Army. Ku Kluxing, like baseball or polo or strip poker, is a pastime pure and simple. Is there not as much boyish fun in dragging a swearing farmer out of his bed at 2 a. m. and smearing him up with tar and the stuffing of a feather sofa pillow as there is in hitting a leather ball with a fat stick or in watching one's friend get down to his last B. V. D. when one draws a flush against his pair? Add to the sport of gumming up the farmer's epidermis the eternal boyish delight in wearing a mysterious badge, a fancy uniform and a romantic mask, and one begins to appreciate the true flavour of Ku Klux frolic. So obvious is the merit of the sport that, in a few years' time, it will have spread all over the North.

§ 30

Human Ingenuity.—Man has invented the telephone, the flying machine, the steamboat, and the automobile. But he has not yet been able to invent a pair of nose glasses that will remain accurately in place, a cure for hay-fever, a sufficiently large umbrella that will roll into convenient shape and size, or a satisfactory soft drink.

§ 31

Pollyanna Note.—The Creator is imperfect deliberately, intentionally. Save He were given to imperfections, millions of His creatures would starve to death. He made the human eye imperfect that thousands of oculists might earn a livelihood; the human foot, that thousands of idiots might live by chiropody; the human finger-nail, that thousands of females might substitute manicuring for street-walking. Through His sapiently manœuvered physical imperfections, thousands of doctors have jobs; through His shrewdly wrought mental imperfections, thousands of shyster lawyers get their bread and butter; through His all-wise manipulation of fatal imperfections He has guaranteed a living even to livery stable owners, florists, campstool manufacturers, black cotton glove merchants, clergymen, bad organists, worse singers, and undertakers.

§ 32

Time Versus Achievement.—Civilization and nature are in ceaseless conspiracy against the man bent seriously upon achievement. Consider the time they compel him to dissipate profitlessly, the hundred and one barriers they interpose between

his goal and the short span of life that is his
wherein to reach it.   Aside from the requirements
of nature—the eight hours of sleep, the considerable periods spent in eating three sustaining
daily meals, the occasional incapacitating illness,
or, more frequently, the spiritual dumps that make
work impossible—there are the countless little
things ordained by civilization to consume his
precious minutes with the jaws of so many vora-
cious wolves: an hour in the mornings spent in
bathing, shaving and dressing, and approximately
the same amount of time spent similarly in the
evenings; the time wasted in getting the hair cut
and in looking after the fingernails; the necessity
for washing the hands a half dozen times between
morning and evening; the social amenities on the
street, over the telephone, and elsewhere—these
are only a few instances.   What is left beyond
these in the day's cycle?   Perhaps six calm, un-
troubled, free hours for one's life's work.   Six
hours for work.   Eighteen wasted.

§ 33

Observation.—I look out of the window of my
writing-room and note three flag-poles on the roofs
of as many high buildings.   The brass balls at
the tops of the poles are immaculately polished.

It occurs to me to speculate on the idiocy of hiring men to climb to the tops of flag-poles on high buildings in order to polish brass balls.

§ 34

A President of the United States.—"I prefer vaudeville," says Woodrow Wilson, "because if an act is bad it is soon over. When a play is bad, the situation is different." A typical example of the Wilsonian reasoning that prevailed during the late war. It is true that if a vaudeville act is bad it is soon over, but what of the succeeding act, and the act after that, and the act still after that? What of them in the aggregate? How many *good* acts has Woodrow seen in all his long experience with vaudeville? Or does he still admire trained seals, Swiss acrobats and xylophone players? "When a play is bad, the situation is different," he says. What is there to prevent him leaving? Or, since the great majority of plays that show in Washington have had a preliminary run in New York, what is there to prevent him from learning about their quality, in advance of his attendance, from the newspapers, magazines or from friends who have seen them? Or, again, which is the safer: to take a chance on *any* play by Shaw, Maugham, Galsworthy, Dunsany, Clare Kummer, Ervine,

Milne, O'Neill, Guitry, Schnitzler, Verneuil, Robinson, Tarkington, one of the Hungarians, Montague Glass, Bahr, Hauptmann, Schönherr, George M. Cohan, Porto Riche or any one of a dozen or more other writers for the current theatre, or on the average vaudeville bill? Doesn't Woodrow yet know the difference in advance between a play by de Caillavet and de Flers and one by the Hattons? Or, in all honesty, isn't his æsthetic taste at bottom chiefly for soft shoe dancers, shimmy shakers, and Eva Tanguay?

§ 35

On Log-Rolling.—I often speculate on the nature of gratification that some men get out of log-rolling in their behalf. A dozen men form a corps for the purpose of mutual back-slapping. One of them produces a cheap piece of work, whereupon the other eleven promptly leap out of their hiding-places in the bushes and proceed frantically to shoot off cologne guns and to illuminate the district for blocks 'round with red fire. How does the recipient of this honour actually regard it? Say he appreciates that his work is cheap work; say that, a year later, he turns out another piece of work that he knows is not cheap work, but very good work, and the

same eleven clowns then again leap out of the same
bushes and shoot off the same cologne and the same
red fire? Is it possible that he isn't completely
disgusted, particularly when he recalls that it is his
duty in return to crouch in the bushes and hold
himself in readiness to hop out and tear off his
undershirt in behalf of any one of his eleven
brothers who seriously elects to make an ass of
himself?

§ 36

The Hate Market.—When I was a boy, they
taught me at school that it was my duty as an
American to hate the English. When I got older,
there was a shift in the market and they told me
that it was my duty as an American to hate the
Spaniards. Then, not long ago, there was another
move and they informed me that it was my duty as
an American to hate the Germans and—a few days
later—the Austrians, the Hungarians, the Bulgari-
ans and the Turks. Now, another shift, and they
are about to tell me that it is my duty as an American to begin hating the Japs. I am an American,
but do not hate the English, the Spaniards, the
Germans, the Austrians, the Hungarians, the Bul-
garians, the Turks or the Japs—and I never did,
and I'm never going to. I am good and damned
sick of this hate business.

§ 37

Prohibition and the Club.—With the advent of Prohibition, the last leg is pulled from under the club. A club without drinks is as much an anomaly as a theatre without a show. The drink is as much a part of a club, and as essential to it, and as vital to its social prosperity, as is a collar button to a shirt. What other reason has a civilized man for entering a club if not to bump a glass with a crony? Take the glass away and the only men you will find in a club are a few imbecile bridge players, a few grafters of free letter paper, and a few men too stingy to buy the *Illustrated London News* and *The Bystander* who hang around the library for a look at them.

§ 38

The Other Fellow's Point of View.—Thus Mr. John Siddall, editor of the *American Magazine,* in an article on "Human Beings":

"I remember a speech on advertising made by a New York advertising man, Mr. Elon G. Pratt. In his speech Mr. Pratt said that some advertisers never seem to learn that in their advertising they talk too much about themselves and not enough about those to whom

they would like to sell their goods.   Then he drove his
point home as follows: 'Too much advertising is written
around the *I* of the advertiser rather than the *you* of the
consumer.'   That remarkable sentence, if taken to heart
and acted on by those who are in need of its teaching,
would be worth millions of dollars.   It often represents the difference between failure and success—not
only in all forms of business but in politics, journalism
and the social relations.   The man who refuses to use
his imagination to enable him to look at things from the
other fellow's point of view simply cannot exercise a
wide influence.   He cannot reach people."

Examples of men who refused to use their imag-
inations to enable them to look at things from the
other fellow's point of view and who therefore
simply could not exercise a wide influence: Chris-
topher Columbus, Napoleon Bonaparte, Otto von
Bismarck, Thomas Jefferson. . . .

§ 39

Lincoln.—The eminently successful pragmati-
cal philosophy of Abraham Lincoln was simply
this: Be complex in politics, incomplex with politicians.

§ 40

Pro Patria.—Despite the sneers of the European

for the American, one will never find him belong-
ing, as the European belongs, to a race of waiters.
The tables in the hotels and restaurants and cafés
of the world are servilely waited on by Englishmen, Irishmen, Frenchmen and Germans, with the
Greeks and Armenians for bus boys, but one is at
pains to find an American wearing an apron, with
a napkin upon his arm, bending to serve fodder.
The American may be, as the European jeers, a
mere tradesman—but you will never find him, like
the Englishman, a butler; or like the Italian, a
bootblack; or like the Frenchman, a headwaiter
with his palm out.

The American is never a headwaiter. But nothing flatters him half so much as a headwaiter's
speaking to him and addressing him by name—
after he has bribed the headwaiter to the condescension with a five-dollar bill.

§ 41

Note on American Society.—I spent the week-
end not long ago at a country house in which the
first butler was addressed by my distinguished host
and charming hostess as *M'sieu.*

§ 42

American Fiction.—The American popular taste in fiction follows the line of American life. That life is one of action, and the taste in fiction thus runs to plot. In Europe, where life is more leisurely and introspective, the taste is more largely for character study. The American has small palate for character study; his reading eye has no time for it; what he wants is a story on six cylinders, with the hero's character designated merely by a policeman's uniform or a Norfolk jacket, and the heroine's merely by diamonds or lack of them.

§ 43

A Dangerous Book.— It is odd that in the prevailing censorship of letters no one has seen fit to note the corruptive, perverting and immoral nature of the classic "Mother Goose." Surely, even to the most liberal and unprejudiced eye, the book contains much that is damaging to the young. It derides marriage (*"Needles and pins, needles and pins, when a man marries, his trouble begins"*). It encourages ignorance (*"Old Mother Goose when she wanted to wander, would ride through the air on a very fine gander"*). It sanctions looseness

(*"Wee Willie Winkie runs through the town, up-stairs and downstairs, in his night-gown"*). It encourages theft—to say nothing of illiteracy—(*"Tom, Tom, the piper's son, stole a pig and away he run"*). It misstates the truth (*"Uphill and down dale, butter is made in every vale"*). It is disrespectful to age and thus encourages bad conduct (*"Ycung lambs to sell! Young lambs io sell! Hear the old man shout and yell!"*). It encourages poaching upon others' rights (*"Little Tommy Tittlemouse lived in a little house, he caught fishes in other men's ditches"*). It is deliberately misleading, and a propagator of false education (*"Jack found, one fine morning, as I have been told, his gocse had laid an egg of pure gold"*). In this last, it is also obviously anti-Semitic. It encourages practises conducive to ill-health (*"Handy, Spandy, Jack-a-Dandy, loves plum cakes and sugar candy"*). It encourages criminal acts (*"I had a little husband no bigger than a thumb, I put him in a pint-pot, etc."*). It condones drunkenness in its approbation of Old King Cole . . .

§ 44

The Moral Republic.—The New York Society for the Suppression of Vice suppresses the best work of Cabell, Dreiser, Moore and Joyce. Mean-

while, on the first pages of the New York newspapers on the day I write are four stories, all re-
lated in sensational detail: (*1*) the story of the
rape of a white woman in Perth Amboy, N. J., by
a negro; (*2*) the description of what occurred in a
bedroom in East Thirty-fifth Street by a woman
witness in the Stokes divorce trial; (*3*) the account
of an alleged affaire between a prominent New
York society woman and a half-breed Indian; and
(*4*) the seduction of a little girl of twelve by an
unfrocked Methodist clergyman in Ohio.

§ 45

L'Après Midi d'un Cabotin.—Not long ago it
befell me to be assigned a room in a hotel next
to one occupied by an actor. The partition between the two rooms was thin, and it was thus that
I was privileged to become privy to the solution
of the mystery as to what an actor does with his
afternoons.

At one o'clock in the afternoon, just as I sat myself down to my second lap in the day's writing
chore, my neighbour arose from his bed, turned on
the water in his tub, and called up a girl. The
telephone conversation lasted exactly fifteen
minutes, and was interrupted only long enough for
my neighbour to turn off the water. After his

bath, my neighbour called downstairs and ordered breakfast, a copy of *Variety*, and two packages of cigarettes. Directly after breakfast, quiet prevailed for half an hour, my neighbour doubtless being engrossed in the literature he had ordered sent up to him. Suddenly, however, a great sound of gaiety filtered through the partition. My neighbour had turned on a phonograph with a jazz record and was executing a pas seul to the strains. A second jazz record followed, and then a sentimental popular "Mammy" ballad. The program completed, my neighbour called up another girl. This conversation, which lasted about ten minutes, was followed by the calling up of still another sweet one, the latter conversation running to fifteen minutes. This eventually concluded, my neighbour called downstairs and ordered up four oranges. A noise of cocktail-shaking ensued presently, and then the gurgle of two beverages.

At three o'clock one of the fair creatures with whom my neighbour had had telephonic communication was announced, and a moment or two later was received in his chamber with a wealth of sweet words. Again the phonograph was turned on, and again a cocktail-shaking fell upon my ears. It developed soon that my neighbour and his fair visitor were practising a particularly intricate dance step. They were—it appeared—going to

an actors' ball at the Ritz that evening, and wished
to display their joint virtuosity before the assembled élite.   Came now presently through the partition endearing phrases and, if my ears deceived
me not, a succession of moist busses.   Again the
cocktail-shaking;   again   the   endearing   phrases;
again   the   succession   of   kisses—and   then—and
then   an   indecipherable   silence   that   lasted   until
quarter of five o'clock.   At this hour my neighbour called up the Lambs' Club and informed a
comrade named Douglas or Donald (I could not
catch the name distinctly) that he would meet him
in twenty minutes and would go with him to tea at
Mrs. Somebody's   house   in   West   104th   Street.
After ten minutes, the sound of a kiss, the slam-
ming of the door by my neighbour and his fair
companion,   the   strains   of   "South   Sea   Moon"
whistled by my neighbour on his way to the ele-
vator—and silence.

§ 46

Auctorial Hocus-Pocus.—About one story in
every fifteen that I encounter treats of a dull con-
glomeration of senseless events the arrant stupidity
and unreadableness of which the author seeks to
mask by tacking on a last line to the effect that
"life, too, is after all just that way: inchoate, inscrutable, meaningless . . ."

§ 47

Constructive Criticism.—(*1*) An exponent of constructive criticism: Hamilton Wright Mabie. (*2*)   An exponent of destructive criticism: Friedrich Wilhelm Nietzsche.

§ 48

Conspiracies.—They speak of the conspiracy of silence by effectual way of killing off a man. There is a surer way.   It is the conspiracy of excessive praise.

§ 49

The Thick Book.—There comes a day in almost every writer's life when he concludes that it is time for him to put solid ground under his reputation by writing a thick book.   A thick book, for some reason or other, is always regarded very seriously by most persons, no matter whether its content is good or bad.   However stupid its matter, it has an air of importance and authority that fetches the general run of people, and the professional critics no less.   Many a writer without particular talent and without an idea worth listening to has gained fame and position by the simple

device of putting out a volume of cyclopedic bulk.
Any book containing 850 pages, printed on heavy
paper and bound sedately in either very dark green
or black cloth is pretty certain to be accepted
with an immense soberness by those who read it
and, even more, by those who merely look at it.
For one man who has actually read Wells' "Outline of History," there are a dozen who consider it
a very great work solely on the ground that, glimps-
ing it in a book-seller's window, they have observed that it weighs about three pounds and is
considerably bigger than anything that Nietzsche
ever published.   It is perhaps safe to say that no
one would ever have taken the late William De
Morgan with one-half the seriousness with which
he was taken had he written novels of the average
length.   What makes Thackeray, Balzac and a
dozen other writers important in the eyes of nine-
tenths of the human race is the fact that each of
them takes up at least four feet on the bookcase
shelf.

Many a writer has gained a reputation on the
weight of a book rather than its contents.   A little
book, however high its merit, is seldom taken with
half the seriousness that is accorded a dull, fat
book.   Shaw, appreciating the fact as all writers
appreciate it, thus confected his "Back to Methu-
selah."   Tedious, turgid, repetitious and often

chaotic though it is, it is certain, by virtue of its enormous heft, to solidify and augment his reputation as none of his small, admirable play books ever did. Its mere size has caused it to be viewed by the majority of readers, playgoers and reviewers solemnly, gravely, and as of paramount significance.

§ 50

Mr. George Horace Lorimer.—Mr. George Horace Lorimer, of the *Saturday Evening Post,* is America's greatest commercial editor. In the entire field of the periodicals there is no editor who can tell so exactly how good a piece of literature it is safe to print without irritating the advertising agent for Stein-Bloch clothes and how bad a piece it is safe to print in order to tickle him. It is this extraordinarily dexterous mid-channel piloting that has made Lorimer's journal what it is, the most successful magazine, financially, in the country. Probably not more than two or three times in the last five years has Lorimer run the risk of printing an incontrovertibly first-rate piece of writing. But, also, probably not more than two or three times in the same period has he run the lesser, but still dangerous, risk of printing a story absolutely and utterly inexcusable. He takes no chances. He obeys the traffic rules as strictly as a baby carriage, and with much the same wistful persuasiveness. Does even one of the favourite houris of his harem do a piece, however good, that might perchance jar the nervous system of little Miss Viviènne Senfgurken, third daughter to August Senfgurken, Fancy Delicatessen, Main and Poplar Streets, Gubyville, Mo., then does he bid the enfant gâté go sell the piece to Munsey. As, for example, in the instance of La Belle Cobb and the tale, "Fish-head." A two million circulation, like the buzz-saw, is something not to be monkeyed with. To give it a philosophy not concurred in by the Inter-Church Movement and the owner of the Silver Dollar Café alike is to court disaster. A two million circulation must have its constant assurance that there is a heaven, that thousands of blind, one-legged newsboys have become bank presidents through their sheer indomitable will, that marriage is the beginning of all happiness, and that it is as great an honour to be superintendent of the Excelsior Suspender Co. as to have composed "Tristan and Isolde." Of this technique, Lorimer is a veritable Houdini. And he has gradually gathered around him a corps of cosmic back slappers, joy spreaders, baby-kissers and gloom perfumers whose pens obediently jump through and lie down at the crack of his golden whip. Some of these pens are of a very considerable intrinsic merit; some of them may be detected in the act of chuckling between the lines while they pocket the easy money. But others, the majority, are the hack pens of the hack magazines, graduated with the degree of L. s. d. It is upon these latter unimaginative pens that the sagacious Lorimer, realizing the truth of the adage "Set a boob to catch a boob," chiefly depends. George Moore, Anatole France and Joseph Conrad compose a less effective triumvirate for the galvanism of Terre Haute and the Campbell Soup advertisement than John Fleming Wilson, H. C. Witwer and Octavus Roy Cohen.

§ 51

The Modern Dances.—The notion, persistently vouchsafed by Methodists, old maids and other such religious orders, that the modern dances are immoral is another of the many ideas that eludes me. The actually immoral dances are not the jazz acrobatics of the moment but the old ones, like the waltz. The present-day quick fox-trots, toddles, shimmies and camel-walks are essentially comic dances—comic no less to the dancers themselves than to the onlookers—and nothing that is comic can be immoral. The old waltz, on the other hand, was a slow, liquorish, insinuating dance, conducive to vagrant thoughts and gipsy fancies. It provoked amorous ideas and amorous feelings. The jazz dances, what their wealth of physical exercise, orchestral din and general hubbub, provoke no more thoughts of a concupiscent nature than a wrestling match.

§ 52

Presidents and Kings.—Many centuries England's junior, it remains that the United States has in its comparatively short career as a nation actually produced more first-rate men as President than England has produced as King. Compare the great Kings of English history with these: George Washington, Thomas Jefferson, Andrew Jackson, Abraham Lincoln, Jefferson Davis, Ulysses S. Grant, and Grover Cleveland.

§ 53

In Memoriam.—The pineapple Daquiri cocktails at the Telegrafo in Havana, the musty ale at the little bar around the corner from the Alhambra in London, the Chateau Haut Brion '09 in the dinky inn near the waterfront at Marseilles, the dark beer in the Mathäserbräu in Munich, the vodka with a dash of peppermint in the café near the jail in Moscow, the Johannisberger Dorf '11 in the Café Bauer in Berlin, the chilled maraschino and brandy at the Café de l'Europe in Vienna, the Tokay up the alley near the railroad station in Budapest, the Bual Madeira in the roadhouse a mile and a half out of Barcelona, the brandy with grated cocoanut on the ships plying between Bahia and Buenos Aires, the Glenlivet Extra Special '88 in the bar to the left of St. Mary's Cathedral in Edinburgh, the pale pink chianti in the café around the corner from Dante's monument in Florence, the crème de rose at Shepheard's in Cairo, the Bronx cocktails at the old Holland House in New York . . .

THE END